11/81

Royal Wedding

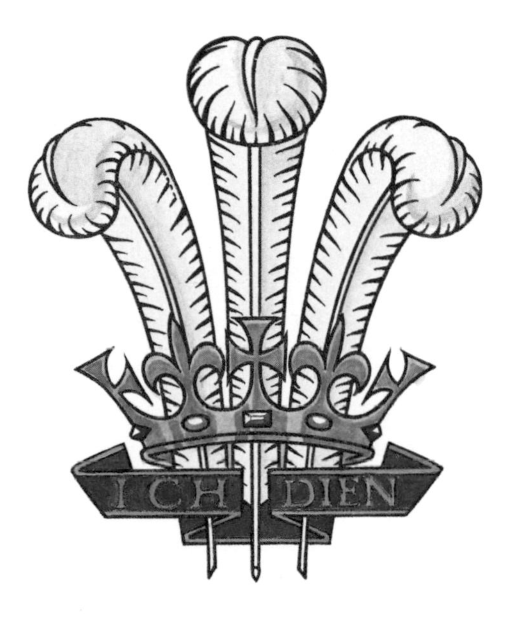

GORDON HONEYCOMBE

Royal Wedding

Michael Joseph and Rainbird

Published in Great Britain by
Michael Joseph Ltd
44 Bedford Square, London WC1, 1981
in association with
The Rainbird Publishing Group Ltd
36 Park Street, London W1Y 4DE
who designed and produced the book

ISBN 0 7181 2088 4

House Editor: Georgina Evans
Designer: Yvonne Dedman

Researcher: Nicholas Courtney

Printed and bound by
Jarrold and Sons Ltd, Norwich, Norfolk

Half-title:
The Prince of Wales' ostrich feathers

Frontispiece:
Prince Charles and Lady Diana Spencer
at Balmoral, 5 May 1981

Contents

Illustration Acknowledgments 6

Author's Acknowledgments 7

1 The Engagement 9

2 The Bride 23

3 The Family of the Bride 37

4 The Bridegroom 57

5 The Friends of the Bride and Groom 81

6 The Families' Weddings 101

7 The Houses of the Prince 111

8 The Princes of Wales 129

9 The Months before the Engagement 147

10 The Weeks before the Wedding 161

11 The Wedding 167

Illustration Acknowledgments

The Rainbird Publishing Group has made every effort to trace the photographers of illustrations used in this book. We apologize if there are copyright holders who have not been acknowledged. On application to Rainbird they will receive a reproduction fee.

The publishers would like to thank the following who have been particularly helpful in supplying pictures and allowing their reproduction in this book:
Reproduced by gracious permission of Her Majesty the Queen: 13, 102–3, 119, 133, 134–5, 136, 138, 138–9, 142–3
The Rt. Hon. The Earl Spencer MVO, Althorp: 37, 38, 42–3, 43, 44, 45, 47 (above and below), 48 (left), 49 (above and below)
Ruth, Lady Fermoy: 52 (above)
Geoffrey Shakerley: 31 (above and below), 54, 108 (above and below)
Tim Graham: frontispiece (2), 8, 20, 34, 35, 42 (above), 56, 76–7, 78, 79, 84–5, 86, 87 (below), 88, 91, 92, 95, 99, 110, 113, 116 (below), 117, 145, 147, 148–9, 151, 152, 154, 155, 156, 160, 161, 164, 166ff

The publishers would also like to thank:
Aerofilms: 118 (below), 153
British Broadcasting Corporation: 18–19
BBC Hulton Picture Library: 129
Beedle & Cooper, Northampton: 49 (above)
John Bethell: 11, 126 (below)
Camera Press Ltd: 22 (Photo: Snowdon), 58 (Photo: Baron), 60 (Photo: John Scott), 96 (Photo: Alan Davidson), 98 (Photo: Patrick Lichfield)
Anthony Carthew: 18–19
The Central Library, King's Lynn: 24 (above), 52 (below), 106 (left)
The Central Press Photos Ltd: 17, 48 (right), 50 (above), 53, 59, 61, 65, 67, 69, 72, 100, 103 (above and below), 104, 106 (right), 107, 122–3, 146, 159, 163 (above and below)
The College of Arms: half-title (1), 40, 63
Mary Evans Picture Library: 130 (left and right), 140
Fox Photos Ltd: 70–1, 75
Eugene Fleury: artwork for family trees on 40–1, 51, 62–3
Keith Graves: 18–19
Peter A. Harding, Tetbury: 114–15
Independent Television News: 18–19
Keystone Press Agency Ltd: 15, 73, 97
Kunsthistorisches Museum, Vienna: 131
London Express News and Feature Services: 10, 116 (above), 157
Mansell Collection: 118 (above), 120–1, 124–5, 144
National Portrait Gallery, London: 39, 132
Norfolk Fire Service: 50 (below)
Reprinted by permission of A.D. Peters & Co. Ltd: 14
Popperfoto Ltd: 68, 105
The Press Association Ltd: 10, 24 (below and below right), 25, 26 (above), 27, 28–9, 166ff
Rainbird Photo Library: Photos: Beedle & Cooper, Northampton – 37, 42–3, 44, 45, 47 (above and below), 48 (left), 49 (below); Photos: David Bradfield – 33, 80; Photos: Goodchild, King's Lynn – 24 (above), 50 (below), 52 (below), 106 (left); Photos: Derrick Witty – 38, 126 (above); 36, 40–1, 51, 62–3
Jamie Robertson: 83
Syndication International: 23, 26 (below), 64 (above and below), 66, 74, 87 (above), 93, 128
Madame Katina Theodossiou: 158
Times Newspapers Ltd: 10
Walker Art Gallery, Liverpool: 36

Illustrations for Chapter 11 on 'The Wedding' were chosen after this page went to press but are acknowledged as occurring on pages 166ff

Author's Acknowledgments

This book has drawn on the writings and remembrances of many people. It would be impossible, and in some cases impermissible, to list all the sources, and a general acknowledgment of my indebtedness and gratitude to all those who have contributed to the writing of the book must suffice: the authors, magazine-writers, journalists, editors, television reporters and correspondents who have covered some of the events herein, and in particular those whose names are commemorated in the text.

I would like to thank the Press Office at Buckingham Palace for their invaluable assistance, and those friends and close relations of the Prince and Princess of Wales whose unique assistance was given with such good faith and good will. But above all I would like to acknowledge my indebtedness and gratitude to Nicholas Courtney, without whose specialized knowledge, industry and enthusiasm I could not have written this book.

Gordon Honeycombe, July 1981

Books and magazines that were particularly helpful included:

George III by Stanley Ayling (Collins, 1972)
Charles, Prince of Wales by Anthony Holden (Weidenfeld and Nicolson, 1979)
Prince Charles, Monarch in the Making by Douglas Liversidge (Arthur Barker, 1975)
HRH Prince Charles by James Whitaker (City Magazine, 1978)
Charles, Prince of our Time by Ronald Allison (Pitkin, 1978)
Charles, In His Own Words compiled by Rosemary York (Omnibus Press, 1981)
Royal Farmers by Ralph Whitcock (Michael Joseph, 1980)
The Girlhood of Queen Victoria 1832–1840 Volume II, edited by Viscount Esher (John Murray, 1912)
Lives of the Queens of England Volume III by Agnes Strickland (Henry Colburn, 1940)
Correspondence of Sarah Spencer, edited by Lady Lyttleton (John Murray, 1912)
George the Fourth by Roger Fulford (revised edition, Gerald Duckworth, 1949)
Heirs Apparent by Thomas Sidney (Alan Wingate, 1957)
A Constitutional King, George the First by Sir Henry Imbert Terry (John Murray, 1927)
Poor Fred, the People's Prince by Sir George Young (Oxford University Press, 1937)
The Princes of Wales by L.G. Pine (Fernhill, 1959)
Queen Victoria, Her Life and Times by Cecil Woodham Smith (Hamish Hamilton, 1972)
A History of Europe by H.A.L. Fisher (Edward Arnold, 1936)
Royal Wedding (IPC Magazines, 1981)
The Royal Wedding Official Souvenir (The Royal Jubilee Trusts, 1981)
Royal Weddings in Vogue 1922–1981 (Condé Nast, 1981)
Tatler (Tatler and Bystander Magazine and Publishing Co.)

CHAPTER 1

The Engagement

'It is with the greatest pleasure that The Queen and The Duke of Edinburgh announce the betrothal of their beloved son, The Prince of Wales, to the Lady Diana Spencer, daughter of the Earl Spencer and the Honourable Mrs Shand Kydd.'

The official announcement was made by Buckingham Palace at 11 a.m. on Tuesday, 24 February 1981, and was flashed by the Press Association around the world at the same time.

In the Palace, the Queen was holding an investiture, the third of six in the early spring, in the red and gilt magnificence of the State Ballroom. Over 150 people had assembled in an ante-room to receive honours and awards, many of which had been announced in the New Year's Honours List. Seated on rows of gilt chairs on the ballroom floor, facing the Yeomen of the Guard and the royal dais, were relatives and friends, who had been entertained with selections of light music played by the Band of the Coldstream Guards in the high gallery behind them. At 11 o'clock a small procession of dark-suited courtiers and Yeomen of the Guard heralded the arrival of the Queen. The Band played the national anthem and everyone rose. At the anthem's conclusion the Queen, standing centrally on the lowest step of the dais, said: 'Please be seated.' The Lord Chamberlain, Lord Maclean, then stepped forward and said: 'The Queen has asked me to let you know that an announcement is being made at this moment in the following terms . . .' Whereupon he read the official notice from the Court Circular. There were gasps from the audience, and then, although they had been advised beforehand not to applaud during the investiture ceremony, some began to clap. Others joined in, and sustained and delighted applause filled the ballroom; the Queen smiled broadly. For those who were there it became an occasion to be remembered in more ways than one.

Prince Charles and Lady Diana Spencer at Buckingham Palace on the afternoon of 24 February 1981

Once before, on 15 November 1977, a departure from the fixed form of the investiture ceremony had occurred when the Queen made an extempore announcement about the birth of her first grandchild, Peter Phillips.

In Church House, Westminster, the Archbishop of Canterbury, Dr Runcie, interrupted a debate on divorce and remarriage at the General Synod of the Church of England, attended by 550 bishops, clergymen and laity, to announce the engagement. Again there was prolonged applause. Later the Archbishop revealed that he had been asked to conduct the marriage service. He said he was 'rather excited about it, and thrilled to be asked . . . As an Archbishop I don't have too many weddings to conduct and I rather miss that side of a priest's ministry.' In the House of Lords, the Lord Chancellor, Lord Hailsham – in the absence of the Lord President, Lord Soames – told the House about the engagement and voiced the congratulations of the peers and bishops; while in the Commons, the Prime Minister, Mrs Thatcher, was asked at question time that afternoon by Christopher Price, Labour MP for Lewisham West, if she would list her official engagements for that day. She replied that she was having an audience with the Queen that night, and said that she would convey the congratulations of the Commons to the Queen, adding that the news of the engagement had brought 'great pleasure' to the Government and MPs of all parties.

Mrs Thatcher had been informed on Monday morning about the engagement, as had the Leader of the Opposition, Mr Foot. The Cabinet was told the same day. Commonwealth heads of state and heads of other governments, as well as the Archbishop of Canterbury, had been informed by coded telegrams. *The Times* was unofficially told, and the paper was able to reveal on that Tuesday morning that: 'The engagement of the Prince of Wales and Lady Diana Spencer is expected to be announced today. The wedding is likely to take place in Westminster Abbey

Tuesday February 24 1981

THE TIMES

Engagement of Prince to be announced today

By a Staff Reporter

The engagement of the Prince of Wales and Lady Diana Spencer is expected to be announced today. The wedding is likely to take place in Westminster Abbey in July.

Lady Diana, aged 19, youngest daughter of Lord Spencer and Mrs Frances Shand Kydd, worked until recently as an assistant in a kindergarten in Pimlico, London.

The Prince of Wales, who is aged 32, once said that he thought "about thirty" was the right age for marriage, and the announcement will bring to an end speculation about the romance that has in recent months put the couple in the centre of press attention.

Lady Diana grew up in circles associated with the Royal Family. Her father was equerry to King George VI and to the Queen, and her name first became known to the public after that of one of her elder sisters, Lady Sarah Spencer, was linked with that of the Prince.

Lady Diana is the youngest of Lord Spencer's four children by his first marriage, to the Hon Frances Roche, daughter of Lord Fermoy.

In 1969 the marriage was dissolved and her mother married Mr Peter Shand Kydd.

Lady Diana returned from Australia last Thursday and was with the Prince the next day when his favourite horse, Allibar, collapsed and died.

PA RUSHFULL
1 Diana (Supersedes ''Charles'')
By Roger Williams, Press Association
Prince Charles is to marry Lady Diana Spencer, Buckingham Palace announced today.
They will wed in the summer, but no date or place has yet been decided the Palace said.
News of the engagement between the 32-year-old heir to the throne and the 19-year-old blonde daughter of Earl Spencer was given exclusively to the Press Association in this brief announcement:
''It is with the greatest pleasure that the Queen and the Duke of Edinburgh announce the betrothal of their beloved son, the Prince of Wales, to the Lady Diana Spencer, daughter of the Earl Spencer and the Honourable Mrs Shand Kydd.''
mf 1102 24/2 fm nnn a 1 diana.

LADY DI AT THE PALACE

Sun picture exclusive

THE Sun

Tuesday, February 24, 1981

Queen and Charles there

By HARRY ARNOLD

LADY Diana Spencer last night paid a mystery visit to Buckingham Palace amid growing speculation that her engagement to Prince Charles is near.

She was accompanied by one of her girlfriends and spent 2½ hours at the Palace.

Mouthed

Both The Queen and Prince Charles were present during the visit—her first to the Palace.

The visit began after 19-year-old Lady Di, whose romance with the Prince was first revealed in The Sun, drove off from her Kensington flat in her Mini-Metro.

As she left her flat she mouthed to waiting photographers: "Don't follow me."

She parked her car in the main forecourt at the front of the Palace close to a sign which said: "Visitors cars only" at about 5.15 and left at around 7.45.

She drove out of the main

Continued on Page 2

in July.' *The Sun*'s exclusive revelations the same morning – 'Lady Diana Spencer went to Buckingham Palace last night amid growing speculation that an announcement of her engagement to Prince Charles was near' – were largely based on a bold interpretation of that visit. Most people in Britain, not as well informed as the readers of *The Times*, heard about the paper's prognostications in the news programmes on commercial and BBC radio.

The tourists who had gathered outside Buckingham Palace to witness the Changing of the Guard at 11.30 a.m. probably failed to appreciate the significance of one tune played by the Band of the Scots Guards: 'Congratulations'. But it was heard by Prince Charles, in his second-floor apartment in the Palace overlooking the forecourt and St James's Park.

Early that morning, the tourists had regarded the activity around three large 5-ton trucks parked outside Green Park gates, with more curiosity than the two guardsmen on sentry duty far across the forecourt. The vans were part of a BBC TV OB (Outside Broadcast) unit: a mobile studio, equipped with a high dish-aerial, cables and electrical equipment, a control room and three studio cameras, one of which was perched on the roof of the leading van. Their presence was due to some clever deduction by the news department at Television Centre.

At 8 a.m., a senior correspondent, Keith Graves, had telephoned the Palace press office to check the story in *The Times* about an engagement announcement. The Palace spokesman was dutifully evasive and non-committal, but when Graves enquired if Michael Shea was there and was told that he was – at 8 a.m. – he guessed something was afoot. For Graves knew that Shea, the Queen's press secretary, had flown the previous week to Oslo, to check on preparations for the Queen's State Visit to Norway at the beginning of May. His tasks completed, Shea had been joined by his Norwegian wife and their children for a family holiday. What happened then was that Michael Shea was telephoned on the Sunday night by the Queen's private secretary, Sir Philip Moore, and told to return to London at once.

Keith Graves was informed by the Palace spokesman that Shea was not available. He aired a personal dilemma: he had arranged to visit his mother that day. The spokesman advised Graves not to go. That was enough for Graves. He telephoned the newsroom and his superiors. At 10 a.m. the Outside Broadcast unit arrived at the Palace; at 10.45 a.m. the BBC and ITN were officially told of the engagement. But it was BBC Television that flashed the news, live, from the pavement opposite the Palace at 11 a.m. with Kate Adie reporting and reading the official announcement.

By this time, the Court correspondents of the Press Association and BBC Radio had been invited to the

Buckingham Palace: tourists and television reporters soon gathered here on the day of the engagement.

Palace to interview the Prince of Wales and his *fiancée* in his private apartment.

Grania Forbes, eight months pregnant and at home on maternity leave, was telephoned at about 10 a.m. by Anne Wall, assistant press secretary to the Queen, and asked to go to the Palace. She arrived three-quarters of an hour later, in time for a briefing in Michael Shea's office, which was adorned with dark, solid furniture, a colour television and paintings chosen by him from the Royal Collection. The briefing was also attended by BBC Radio's Court correspondent, David McNeil. They were handed a typed list of six prepared questions by Shea and discussed what other questions they would like to ask. Both interviewers wanted to enquire about the age gap between the Prince and Lady Diana. Shea said he would check this with the Prince. He then took them up in a lift to the second floor of the Palace, through a long red-carpeted corridor, lined with paintings, sofas, tables and cabinets containing priceless porcelain, which overlooked the inner courtyard, to a large white painted door, where they were briefly left while Shea entered the Prince's apartments and cleared the additional questions with him. After a short wait, Grania Forbes was invited into the Prince's private sitting-room, where he had proposed to his future bride.

At 11.35 a.m., Prince Charles and Lady Diana entered the room from an inner door. The Press Association's Court correspondent, heavily pregnant in her black maternity dress, managed a graceful curtsey. She offered the couple her congratulations and all three sat down, the Prince and his *fiancée* on a sofa, while Grania Forbes perched on an arm chair opposite them with a notepad at hand. After a few preliminaries, the interview began.

It was the first interview that Lady Diana had ever given. Dressed in a ruby-red velvet suit, with a matching red-and-white patterned shirt ruffled at the neck, red stockings and shoes, she was composed, but shy; she spoke little and sometimes blushed. She was not shy, however, about displaying her engagement ring, a large oval sapphire set with fourteen diamonds on a platinum ring, said to have cost in the region of £28,500. The ring was made by Garrard & Co., Crown Jewellers, of Regent Street, and had been chosen by Lady Diana herself.

She had been up since 7.30 a.m., having woken in the unaccustomed surroundings of a bedroom in Clarence House, the Queen Mother's London residence, into which she had moved the night before. At

8.15 that morning she was driven by her sister, Lady Jane Fellowes, to Thurloe Street in South Kensington, to her hairdresser's, Head Lines, for an 8.30 a.m. appointment. Her favourite hairdresser, Kevin Shanley, a twenty-six-year-old Londoner, had opened up the salon especially for her and guessed that her early visit must have a very special reason. 'I had an idea,' he said afterwards, 'because she said it was a special day.' He gave her hair his best attention for an hour, during which she telephoned her eldest sister, Lady Sarah. She then returned to Clarence House to change and was in Buckingham Palace, with the Prince in his apartments, when the official announcement was made.

He had been in the Palace since Friday. He was dressed that Tuesday morning in a grey, single-breasted suit. During the interview with Grania Forbes, the first of three he and Lady Diana gave that day, he encouraged his *fiancée* to reply to questions by inviting her opinion and giving her reassuring and affectionate looks. There was no sense of strain; both seemed happy and pleased. In the background stood the Prince's private secretary, the Hon. Edward Adeane. Occasionally he exchanged words with Michael Shea. The sound of traffic racing around the Victoria Memorial dimly penetrated the long, double-glazed sitting-room windows – as did the brassy melodies of the Band of the Scots Guards.

The Prince was affable and expansive: he had met Grania Forbes before and had last been interviewed by her in 1977. He answered her questions freely.

'I'm positively delighted and frankly amazed,' said Prince Charles, 'that Diana's prepared to take me on.'

Grania asked when the wedding would be. The wedding day, he said, would probably be in the second half of July.

She asked him when he had proposed. 'I asked Diana just before she went to Australia.' He continued: 'I wanted to give her a chance to think about it – to think if it was all going to be too awful.'

Lady Diana interposed: 'Oh, I never had any doubts about it.'

The difficult part, he added, was keeping the news a secret and their excitement to themselves.

Neither could really remember meeting before November 1977. Lady Diana said: 'Prince Charles came to shoot. He was really a friend of my sister then.'

The Prince remembered her as being 'a splendid sixteen-year-old . . . I remember thinking what fun she was.'

Their romance began when Lady Diana went to Balmoral in July 1980. 'We began to realize then that there was something in it,' said Prince Charles.

No decisions, he said, had yet been taken about the honeymoon. 'We've discussed vague ideas,' he explained, 'and now people might come up with suggestions of where we might go.'

They had not decided yet where they would live. 'I have only two rooms here and a bedroom,' Prince Charles remarked, 'so it will obviously be difficult to stay here for very long.' He added that their main base would be at Highgrove, his Gloucestershire home.

Grania Forbes asked Lady Diana if she had got the house organized yet. She replied: 'Not quite yet.'

'It's just like camping,' explained the Prince. 'We've only got one room decorated downstairs, and the bedroom organized. Otherwise, everything is being painted. There's nothing there yet – no curtains, carpets or furniture. Nothing.'

When asked about the age-gap, Lady Diana replied: 'I haven't really thought about it – although at one stage I always ganged up with Prince Andrew.'

Prince Charles replied: 'It's only twelve years. Lots of people have got married with that sort of age difference. I just feel you're only as old as you think you are . . . Diana will certainly keep me young . . . I think I shall be exhausted!' He went on to say that she would make a very good Princess of Wales. 'I'm sure she'll be very, very good . . . She'll be twenty soon, and I was about that age when I started. It's obviously difficult to start with, but you just have to take the plunge.'

'I'll just take it as it comes,' commented his *fiancée*.

Both said they were 'thrilled' about the engagement. 'We're only sad,' said Prince Charles, 'that Lady Diana's mother can't be here as she's stuck in Australia.' He also said he was sorry he had had to cancel a visit to the Foreign and Commonwealth Office that morning, where he would have continued his studies of government and business. He grinned happily: 'I've always wanted to throw a spanner in the works of my programme. Today I think I've managed to throw in a crowbar.'

They outlined what they felt they had in common. 'We both love music and dancing,' said Lady Diana, 'and we both have the same sense of humour.'

Prince Charles laughed and said: 'You'll definitely need that!'

Grania Forbes commented on his *fiancée*'s poise and confidence. Lady Diana conceded that it was 'marvellous' to have Prince Charles's support. She said: 'It's always nice when there are two of you and there's someone there to help you.'

At the end of the half-hour interview all three stood. 'Thank-yous' were exchanged and before

The Grand Staircase, Buckingham Palace. This staircase gives access to the main state apartments, including the Ballroom, where the Queen held an investiture on 24 February 1981.

Grania Forbes left the room the Prince enquired when her baby was due and wished her well. Her baby arrived four weeks later: a boy christened Edward.

The Press Association's Court correspondent was replaced by that of BBC Radio, David McNeil. While he recorded his interview in the Prince's sitting-room, Lady Diana's father, Earl Spencer, was being interviewed by two television reporters attached to the two Outside Broadcast units parked in front of the gates of Green Park.

Kate Adie had been joined among the crowd of tourists by Keith Hatfield of ITN, who had spent the morning, since 7 a.m. doorstepping Coleherne Court, the block of flats where Lady Diana lived. A large posse of pressmen and photographers, primed by their editors should *The Times*' forecast prove to be correct, had gathered in the cold, wet street – it had rained earlier and would snow later that afternoon. Many had arrived after learning at 10 o'clock that Prince Charles's scheduled visit to the Commonwealth and Foreign Office had been postponed. Their suspicions were further aroused when Lady Diana's three flatmates left Coleherne Court late for work – at half-past ten – and seemed unusually merry. But it was the subsequent appearance of the janitor and his Irish assistant in their best suits, of two immaculate police officers in the lobby, and of a coachload of policemen who debussed in a side street before blanketing the block, that set the newshounds racing for their cars and the nearest telephones. Some drove to Buckingham Palace to see what was happening outside – as did Earl Spencer and his second wife, Countess Spencer, who brought along with them her twelve-year-old son by her first husband, the Earl of Dartmouth. Earl Spencer had brought a Leicaflex camera with him. He told reporters: 'We came here because I wanted to photograph the photographers. I've photographed every important event in Diana's life, and I wanted to record this one as well.' He might have passed unnoticed had not Keith Hatfield thought the woman in the white mink hat and coat with him looked like Barbara Cartland. In fact she is her daughter.

Confusion reigned for some moments as the two television crews descended on Earl Spencer and his wife. Spectators crowded around.

Kate Adie was the first to talk to the Earl: 'Well – can I say "Congratulations", Earl Spencer?' she enquired.

'Very proud. Very happy,' he replied. His voice was slightly slurred – an after-effect of the stroke he had suffered in 1979, a week after a party he had given to celebrate the final payment of the death-duties

SUNDAY 1 MARCH 1981

TELEVISION by Clive James

On the Charles trail

PURPLE TUESDAY was the most stunning event in the history of the British monarchy since King Harold got hit in the eye with an arrow. By the time the sirens had stopped howling, all the television channels were at action stations and pumping out special programmes like a pom-pom barrage.

Frank Bough was in charge at **Nationwide** (BBC1). Large photographs of Prince Charles and Lady Diana were behind him. Around him were some plants. Casually but neatly attired, he had the air of one who knows how to stay calm when the crisis bursts. 'So at last the long wait is over . . . we'll be telling you more . . . start by going over to Hugh Scully, standing in front of the building which has been at the heart of today's events.' Frank meant Buckingham Palace, in front of which Hugh Scully was now discovered to be standing, accompanied by several hundred sightseers and some falling snow.

It was cold and dark, but Hugh was undaunted. 'People waiting to catch a glimpse . . . that hasn't happened . . . we can't actually see . . . the floodlights have not actually been switched *on*.' The bits of Hugh that were inside his sheepskin-lined car-coat were probably quite cosy, but his face was stiffening while you watched. Nevertheless he managed to prise a vox pop out of a nearby woman, who explained how she planned to stay warm during what promised to be an all-night vigil. 'I put two of everything on . . . stay up overnight.' 'Is it worth it ?' croaked Hugh. 'Oh yes. Television's not the *same* . . . wonderful, very nice girl.' 'It is quite *cold*, isn't it ?' asked Hugh at random, like someone reciting poetry while freezing to death on Everest.

Back to Frank in the nice comfy studio, where he had a theory about why Charles and Diana had not appeared on the balcony. 'I think they're both inside cracking a bottle of champagne . . . highly significant day in the history of the British monarchy.' Sue Cook appeared, with three little ducks flying up the shoulder of her pullover. 'It was while he was at Cambridge,' Sue told us, 'that Charles really first discovered girls for the first time.' There followed a comprehensive survey of the girls, culminating in the one who 'could literally be the girl next door.' This last assurance was accompanied by a photograph of next door. There was also a picture of Barbara Cartland, perhaps to galvanise anybody in the audience who had been tending to nod off.

'Amongst our guests tonight,' Frank announced, 'is Harry Herbert, a life-long friend of Lady Diana. What's she really like ?' 'She's terrific . . . leads the outdoor life . . . lot of sport. . . .' 'She's had some good friends in these past few months,' ventured Frank, meaning those flat-mates who had fought off the media. 'Does she have the kind of personality that can withstand that glare . . . pressure . . . publicity ?' Tina Brown, editor of the *Tatler*, was there to agree that Lady Diana had what it took to ward off the intrusive Press. 'She's absolutely trained for it. And so are her friends.'

Sue Cook reviewed the activities of 'some of the world's most highly trained newshounds.' Prominent among these was the exceptionally highly trained James Whitaker of the *Daily Star*. Whitaker has been on the Charles trail for yonks, but has not grown cynical. Quite the reverse. Plainly he is besotted by Lady Diana. 'I think she likes me . . . I have been very intrusive now for five or six years.' Whitaker said all this while wearing binoculars and standing in a phone booth, presumably to demonstrate his outstandingly high state of training.

It was made clear that the British Press, however highly trained its news-hounds might be, was a model of discretion compared to the foreign Press. Sandro Paternostro and his very thin moustache were adduced as representatives of

Frank Bough : Dazzled by genealogy.

Italian television. 'They are like fairy tales,' trilled Sandro, adding something about 'psychological escape from the gloomy of everyday's life.' You could see why Frank fancies himself to be a cut above that sort of thing. 'I bet she's glad to be well rid of *that* lot,' he scoffed, obviously never contemplating the possibility that she might be offering up prayers to be well rid of him too.

'Let's join Hugh Scully,' Frank suggested, 'and of course he's still standing outside Buckingham Palace.' By now Hugh was frozen into position like Shackleton's ship in the pack ice. 'It's now snowing quite heavily . . . hoping for a glimpse . . . snow . . . cold.' An Australian lady standing in the drift next to him was more ebullient. 'I'm so glad I'm here for this occasion. It's been the highlight of my trip.' Back to Frank. '*Marvellous* people down there at the Palace this evening,' he crooned snugly, settling further back in his soft leather chair. It wasn't snowing where Frank was. The North West plugged in. 'She seems a noice enough gurrul, you know,' said a rude mechanical from Dufton, but obviously the Prince's absenteeism had given rise to a certain lack of gruntle in the locals. 'Do you think you'll see a lot of them ?' 'Well, if we don't see more of him than we do we won't see much.'

An expert on royalty called Audrey suggested it might be a quiet wedding. 'Very swish wedding ?' asked Frank. 'What ?' 'Swish.' 'Oh yes, very swish.' Someone going under the name of Hugh Montgomery-Massingberd dazzled Frank with a lot of science about genealogy. 'All four grandparents . . . links with godparents.' 'You've just about lost me,' frowned Frank, but perked up when the bride's father appeared and immediately established himself as a hit act. 'He asked my permission, which was rather sweet of him. Wonder what he would have said if I'd said no.'

The Earl belted on as if P. G. Wodehouse had invented him. 'Diana's life has been very difficult. No protection at all. Very grateful for those girls in her flat. Incidentally, when she was a baby she was a superb physical specimen.' The Earl was hastily supplanted by a filmed interview with none other than the magic couple, so there was an opportunity to check up straight away on the current state of the superb physical specimen. She looked just fine. They were asked what they had in common. 'What a difficult question,' mused the Prince. 'Sport . . . love of the outdoors.'

At about this time a Thames Special started up on the commercial channel, with Peter Sissons in charge. The show began with the same interview, so you got two chances to watch the happy couple. 'We sort of met in a ploughed field,' said Lady Diana, and in the background you could hear the roar of accelerating Land-Rovers as the highly trained newshounds headed up-country to get pictures of the ploughed field. In the foreground was a close-up of the Prince scratching Lady Diana's hand. Or else it was his own hand—it was hard to figure out which fingers were whose, a conundrum which only added to the charm.

'Can you find the words to sum up how you feel today ?' the digitally entwined twain were asked. 'Difficult. Delighted . . . happy." And, I suppose, in love ?' The Prince looked as if he had just found Sandro Paternostro hiding under his bed, but did his best to find an answer. Cut to Keith Hatfield outside Buckingham Palace. Spattered by those few flakes of snow which had not already accumulated on Hugh Scully, Keith tried to snatch an interview from the bride's parents as they left. 'Don't talk about it,' the Earl instructed his wife. 'We've just done it. Just talked to the BBC and ITN about it.' The Countess found a more gracious way of fobbing Keith off. 'So many imponderables,' she said evasively.

Meanwhile 'Nationwide' was winding up. 'Almost all,' said Sue Cook, 'but first back to Hugh Scully in front of Buckingham Palace.' Lit by a sun-gun in the chill darkness, Hugh looked like Scott of the Antarctic several weeks after making the last entry in his diary. 'Crowds outside the Palace now beginning to disperse as it becomes clear that they are unlikely to get a glimpse . . . cold . . . and happy day.'

Clive James reviews the television coverage of the engagement in the 'Observer' on Sunday, 1 March 1981.

The Earl and Countess Spencer mingled with the crowds outside Buckingham Palace on the day of the engagement.

incurred by his father's demise. Keith Hatfield said later that the Earl seemed perplexed, almost overwhelmed, bemused by the fact that he was being interviewed for television.

Kate Adie, controlling her delighted amazement at encountering the Earl, asked him: 'What are you doing on the pavement *outside* the Palace? I thought you'd be *inside*.'

'I've been posing for the photographers,' he replied.

'Oh, what a marvellous day for you!' she exclaimed, for once almost at a loss for words.

He replied: 'Lovely day. Lovely day. We're all very happy. I saw Diana last night. She was looking absolutely radiant. Radiant – and very happy. Never seen her look better.'

He described how Prince Charles had telephoned him and asked for his youngest daughter's hand in marriage. The Earl remarked: 'I don't know what he would have said if I'd turned him down.' He added: 'I'm delighted for her. Publicity doesn't worry her . . . She's very practical and down to earth, and a very good housewife.'

'We're very happy and proud,' said Countess Spencer. 'Very pleased it's all resolved. I think we both feel enormously proud of Diana, that she's taking on such a big responsibility. And she's also a great giver, you know. She's a very generous kind of person. She wants to give rather than take, and that, I think, is most important of all. Don't you?'

Both the Spencers were then interviewed by Keith Hatfield, after which the bride-to-be's father, her step-mother and step-brother, Henry, were swallowed up in the autograph-seeking crowd, and made their way back to the gold-coloured Rolls Royce by which they had arrived.

Most of the crowd, fascinated by the Outside Broadcast units, by all the activity around the television cameras, were still uncertain what was happening or what had happened. Quite a few were foreign; most were tourists. But by lunchtime several hundred people had gathered at the gates of the Palace, disposed to cheer and wave, despite the cold.

Inside the Palace, Prince Charles and Lady Diana were having lunch with the Queen in her first floor apartments overlooking the Palace gardens. Prince Andrew was also there. His twenty-first birthday had been on the previous Thursday, and he had celebrated the occasion at Windsor Castle that weekend. When he heard about the engagement, he obtained a brief extension of his leave – he was attending a helicopter pilot's course at the Royal Navy Air Station at Culdrose – and went to Buckingham Palace.

After lunch, Lady Diana changed into another suit for her first official appearance with her *fiancé*. Bought at Harrods and designed by Cojana, a British fashion-house which had won a Queen's award the previous year, the sapphire, scalloped-edged suit and bow belt were made of pure silk; the white blouse and scarf were imprinted with a blue swallow motif. Prince Charles remained in the suit he had worn that morning. At one time it was thought the Queen might appear with the couple, but she decided to stay in the background and not take any of the limelight away from them: it was their day.

A photo-call for press photographers and television cameras had been arranged for 3 p.m. The venue was the terrace and lawn at the rear of the Palace, where every summer garden-parties with hundreds of guests are held. On that damp and cold February afternoon, eight photographers, representatives of the main news organizations and agencies in Britain, assembled with television crews from the BBC and ITN. They were given about twelve minutes to find and snap the happiest, most natural pose that might be used around the world to commemorate the engagement.

The Prince and Lady Diana emerged arm-in-arm from the Palace promptly at 3 o'clock, attended by four soberly suited courtiers: Sir Philip Moore, Edward Adeane, Bill Heseltine, the Queen's deputy private secretary, and Michael Shea. No equerry was in attendance. The Prince and his *fiancée* were encouraged by the photographers to pose on the terrace steps, to walk along the lawn, to do everything more than once and always with a smile. Lady Diana bashfully and briefly obeyed a request to lay her head on the Prince's shoulder, to a chorus of: 'That's it! Fantastic! Great!'

It was observed by the two television correspondents covering the occasion, Anthony Carthew of ITN and Keith Graves of the BBC, that the couple, despite the artifice and awkwardness of the occasion, seemed fairly relaxed, were even quite jolly, and were pleased to walk up and down and pose for the photographers. It was noted that Lady Diana, despite her flat shoes, was nearly as tall as her *fiancé*. The Queen, like any mother on such a day, was observed to be watching the scene, peering through the curtains of her apartments. On being observed, she smiled and withdrew.

By 3.15 p.m. the photo-call was brought to an end by Michael Shea and the photographers dismissed. It was now time for the television interview.

The interviewers, Carthew and Graves, had earlier persuaded Mr Shea that his list of agreed questions should be expanded into a conversation; he was assured that neither interviewer would ask the wrong questions. They suggested that the interview should be conducted indoors, where it would be warmer and the couple more relaxed, and not outside as planned. So the television crews, the courtiers and the engaged couple moved off the terrace into the Bow Room, a high, largely empty room with tall mirrors and two fireplaces. One of them, topped by a huge gilt mirror, was chosen as a background, and bowls of flowers were fetched to stand on side-tables to decorate the scene. As lights, sound equipment and the cameras were positioned, a delay was caused by the unforeseen fact that the Palace had round-point sockets, not square ones.

The interviewers chatted with the Prince of Wales and Lady Diana, while the courtiers stood in the background. Both Carthew and Graves were struck by the sense of release, the euphoria that the Prince and his *fiancée* seemed to feel. They had both met him before and remarked how relaxed he was, unselfconsciously clasping Lady Diana's hand, eagerly asking what they thought about the engagement. 'Were you surprised?' he enquired, referring to its timing. The decision to make the announcement, he said, had been influenced by his forthcoming visit to New Zealand and Australia. He favoured a wedding in July because, he said, he could not stand autumn weddings. The interviewers thought Lady Diana was very good-looking and stylish. Carthew was intrigued by the saucy way she lowered her head and looked up at them under the sweep of her hair. She smiled happily but admitted to feeling nervous. '*You're* nervous! *We're* nervous!' exclaimed Graves. The couple were assured that the interviewers, who would ask alternate questions, were as keen to make the interview a good one as the couple themselves. 'If you're not happy,' they were told, 'say so and we'll stop.' But the only break that occurred was when the video-cassette on one of the latest electronic news gathering cameras had to be changed.

Prince Charles and Lady Diana pose for photographers on the terrace steps at Buckingham Palace on their engagement day.

The Television Interview

Interviewers: Can you remember when you first met?

Lady Diana: Yes . . . yes. I think I can. It was 1977. Prince Charles came to stay as a friend in my sister's house for a shoot, and we sort of met in a ploughed field.

Interviewers: What did you think then? What was your instant impression – both of you?

Prince Charles: Well, I remember thinking what a very jolly and amusing and attractive sixteen-year-old she was. I mean, great fun – bouncy and full of life and everything. *(To Lady Diana)* I don't know what you thought of me, but —

Lady Diana: Pretty amazing.

Interviewers: What in fact do you think you have in common?

Prince Charles: It's a difficult question. *(To Lady Diana)* What do you think we've got in common?

Lady Diana: Sense of humour – every outdoor activity. Except I don't ride.

Prince Charles: We'll soon remedy that.

Lady Diana: Lots of things really.

Interviewers: What about you, Sir?

Prince Charles: Um, certainly all sorts of things . . . Our love of the outdoors. And she's a very energetic character as well – which is very encouraging. Music, and interests like that, and skiing. She's a great skiier – although I haven't seen her skiing yet.

Interviewers: Is she better than you?

Prince Charles: Well, I don't know. But my philosophy is to go down the hill as fast as I can, and I'm sure yours is too *(to Lady Diana)*. Isn't it?

Lady Diana: I never turn. *(They both laugh)*

Interviewers: It must have been a tremendous strain in the past few months for you, and now all of a sudden you can come and stand in front of the cameras hand-in-hand. Has it been a strain trying to carry out a courtship without anyone knowing?

Lady Diana: Yes, it has. But anyone in the position we've been in would feel the pressure and everything. But it's been worthwhile, every bit of it.

Interviewers: The Prince has been in this position all his life. It was something that was entirely new to you of course?

Lady Diana: Yes, but I hope I coped all right. I'm still around anyway.

Interviewers: I think we're all full of admiration for the way you did cope, if I may say so . . . What about the proposal, Your Royal Highness – how did that come about?

Prince Charles: Um, well, I asked Diana before she went to Australia – two or three days before – because I thought it would be a good idea that, apart from anything else, if she went to Australia she could then think about it. And if she didn't like the idea, she could say she didn't or she did. But in fact she said *(to Lady Diana)* . . . You know what you said?

Lady Diana: 'Yes' – quite promptly.

Interviewers: Before you went to Australia?

Lady Diana: Yes.

Prince Charles: I said you had better sit on it for three weeks.

Interviewers: It must have been an agonizing three weeks. Did you speak at all? I mean, the telephone lines must have been pretty busy between here and Australia.

Prince Charles: Yes, we tried. But it was quite difficult, because I think there was a certain amount of press interest there, although they never actually found you, did they?

Lady Diana: No.

Prince Charles: I rang up on one occasion and I said: 'Can I speak — ?' And they said: 'No, we're not taking any calls'. So I said: 'It's the Prince of Wales speaking'. 'How do I know it's the Prince of Wales?' came back the reply. I said: 'You don't. But I am', in a rage. And eventually . . . I mean, I got the number because they were staying somewhere else. They said the phones were tapped or something – which I found highly unlikely. . . .

Interviewers: Did it cross either of your minds in 1977 that one day you would be announcing your engagement?

Both: No. No, not at all.

Interviewers: At what point did you decide that this was the right lady for *you*?

Prince Charles: Gradually . . . I suppose towards the end of the summer and autumn last year. I began to realize what was going on in *my* mind, and hers in particular, and all these things helped. But it was a gradual business.

Interviewers: Did *you* find it a very hard decision, Lady Diana?

Lady Diana: I had a long time to think about it . . . but it wasn't a difficult decision in the end. It was what I wanted – it's what I want.

Interviewers: I haven't seen the ring. May we have a look at it?

Lady Diana: Yes. It's a wonderful sapphire, and diamonds.

Interviewers: When were you given that? Just last night?

Lady Diana: No – Sunday.

Interviewers: But you weren't wearing it yesterday?
Lady Diana: No . . . Hidden.
Interviewers: When did you tell the Queen that this was what you wanted to do?
Prince Charles: Well, about three weeks ago. So, as I say, we've had to sit on it and hide it for three weeks – which hasn't been all that easy. But I was absolutely determined that it was going to be as near a secret as possible on the actual day. That was my ambition.
Interviewers: It must have been awfully difficult trying to keep that secret.
Prince Charles: Yes.
Lady Diana: Very good for us.
Interviewers: Very good practice.
Prince Charles: And good for the people we told too. Quite interesting to see who can keep secrets.
Interviewers: But it did pop up in *The Times* this morning. Someone talked to the right newspaper.
Prince Charles: What they call the top people's newspaper.
Interviewers: No announcement yet of where and when?
Prince Charles: You mean the date of the wedding? No, because there's a lot to be decided. *When* is probably in the latter half of July, I should think. It's, I think, quite a useful time – for all sorts of different reasons. And the actual place will soon be decided.
Interviewers: Honeymoon plans? Or is that something you have to talk about now it's official?
Prince Charles: Well, we've had vague discussions about it. But a lot depends, you know, on what happens now. There are lots of alternatives. Everybody should go somewhere where one can actually get away from everything else.
Interviewers: Having puzzled over the decision, you are now going to be separated again – because you're going to Australia and New Zealand. And you'll be away – what? – five, six weeks? Something like that.
Prince Charles: Yes.
Interviewers: *(To Lady Diana)* What are you going to do in the meantime?
Lady Diana: Don't worry, I shall be very busy.
Interviewers: Not back to the nursery and not back to flat-sharing, presumably?
Lady Diana: No.
Interviewers: You've moved to your accommodation?
Lady Diana: I'll be moving all over the place, I should think.
Interviewers: You'll miss looking after the children?
Lady Diana: Yes.
Prince Charles: They'll certainly miss you, won't they?
Lady Diana: Hope so.
Interviewers: Have you been to see them and told them the news?
Lady Diana: No.
Interviewers: It would have been a bit of a give-away.
Prince Charles: The moment you appear anywhere, people automatically jump to conclusions.
Interviewers: Well, now that you can appear in public, it must be a great relief to you.
Prince Charles: It is rather.
Interviewers: *(To Lady Diana)* Do you find it daunting? – That yesterday you were a nanny, looking after children, and now you're about to marry the Prince of Wales, and one day will in all likelihood be Queen. It's a tremendous change for someone, if I may say, of nineteen to make such a sudden transition.
Lady Diana: It is – but I've had a small run-up to it all in the last six months, and next to Prince Charles I can't go wrong. He's there with me.
Interviewers: Are you planning for the future? You must be planning for the future – where you're going to live and that sort of thing?
Prince Charles: Oh, yes, yes, yes. I've got this house in Gloucestershire, which I acquired last year.
Interviewers: With marriage in mind?
Prince Charles: No. No, not really. I mean, I did want somewhere very much as a base, and I wanted somewhere which was near the Duchy of Cornwall areas . . . And so that was very convenient. But there's a lot to be done. It'll be marvellous to have somebody to help sort it out.
Interviewers: Lady Diana's father described her this morning as – he said he thought she'd make a very good housewife.
Prince Charles: We've yet to see!
Interviewers: Can you find the words to sum up how you feel today – both of you?
Prince Charles: Difficult to find the words, really – *(to Lady Diana)* isn't it? Just delighted and happy. I'm amazed that she's been brave enough to take me on.
Interviewers: And I suppose in love?
Lady Diana: Of course!
Prince Charles: Whatever 'in love' means.
Interviewers: It obviously means two very happy people. Well – from us – congratulations.
Both: Thank you very much.

The interview lasted fifteen minutes in all. Graves and Carthew stood side by side opposite the Prince of Wales and his *fiancée* with the BBC and ITN camera crews on either side of them.

Afterwards, the Prince enquired: 'How did it go?' and added: 'I thought it seemed to go very well.' Graves and Carthew agreed; they complimented Lady Diana on being so natural. For a few minutes the four chatted together. Then the Prince, probably quite relieved that this particular interview, more personal in a way than any other he had given, was over, prepared to leave. He shook hands with the interviewers, thanked them and the crews and moved away. Lady Diana, chatting to Carthew, was caught unawares by the Prince's departure, until she suddenly realized that he had stopped to wait for her by the door and that the courtiers stood waiting for her to precede them. She giggled, shrugged and smiled, and marched over to the Prince. He grinned at her and they left the room hand in hand.

By now it was after 4 o'clock. Outside the Palace, the large crowd (too small, however, to merit a balcony appearance) stood and stared at its façade, darkening in the winter afternoon as the day waned. It began to get even colder. They stared at the empty balcony, at windows in which lights began to appear, and their patience was at last rewarded when in the dusk, made bright at the gates by television lights, a car whisked out of the forecourt with the Prince's smiling *fiancée* inside. She was driven to Clarence House, where that night she and the Prince of Wales dined with their respective grandmothers, Lady Fermoy and Queen Elizabeth the Queen Mother, who more than most had fondly watched and wondered for many months, hoping this wished-for union of their families would one day be made fact.

The evening of the 24 February was spent having dinner at Clarence House with the Queen Mother and Lady Fermoy.

Afterwards, the Prince and his *fiancée* emerged from the house to wave at the crowd outside, whose joyful applause and cheering put the seal on what had been for all concerned a most unusual and happy day.

Left: Queen Elizabeth the Queen Mother

CHAPTER 2

The Bride

Lady Diana Spencer was born on 1 July 1961 on the afternoon of a very warm day, said to have been the hottest summer afternoon for fifteen years. Her father was Viscount Althorp, aged thirty-seven, heir to the 7th Earl Spencer, and her mother, Viscountess Althorp, aged twenty-five, was formerly the Hon. Frances Roche, youngest daughter of Lord and Lady Fermoy. The birth took place in Park House on the Sandringham estate, a few hundred yards from the Royal Family's Norfolk home, and in the very room in which the baby's mother herself had been born in January 1936.

The Althorps, who had married in June 1954 in Westminster Abbey, already had two children, both daughters, then aged six and four. A third child, a son, had died at birth in January 1960, and the Althorps had hoped for a son. Indeed, no particular names had been chosen for the new arrival. Her father said later: 'She was a delightful child, and as a baby she could have won any beauty competition.' She was christened at Sandringham Church by a former Bishop of Norwich and named Diana Frances after a Spencer ancestress and her mother. A son, Charles, was born to the Althorps three years later.

At the time of Lady Diana's birth, Prince Charles was a twelve-year-old schoolboy, a boarder at Cheam Preparatory School in Hampshire.

Lady Diana's childhood was spent at Park House. Later, she would say: 'I feel my roots are in Norfolk. I have always loved it there.' Much of her time was spent outside in play; family pets abounded: horses, dogs (springer spaniels) and hamsters. She was particularly fond, her mother says, 'of anything in a small cage'. Childhood illnesses and mishaps were few; she was a trouble-free, happy child.

Her nanny was a girl from Kent, Judith Parnell, and in 1965, when Lady Diana was four, she acquired a governess, Miss Gertrude Allen, who had also tutored her mother when she was a child. Miss Allen, who died recently, taught Lady Diana to read and write, and remembered her as being a 'relaxed' child and 'a tidy soul'. As to learning, she was 'conscientious' and 'a real trier'. She was fond of soft toys, according to her father: 'She loved her soft toys nearly as much as she loved babies. She always loved babies.' She was also fond of stories; it is said that even then she was interested in history – particularly as her next-door neighbours, whom she saw coming and going for brief periods in the summer and winter, were a queen, princesses and princes. One prince, a rumbustious, handsome little boy, called Andrew, was only a year and a half older. Not surprisingly, although the royal neighbours held a certain

Left: Lady Diana Spencer photographed by Lord Snowdon

Right: Lady Diana held by her mother at her christening in 1961 while her father looks on

Above: Park House, Sandringham, where Lady Diana spent her childhood

Below: Lady Diana, at Park House, on her first birthday

Right: Lady Diana at Park House

Opposite page: A drawing of Lady Diana, aged four, by Madame Pawlikowska

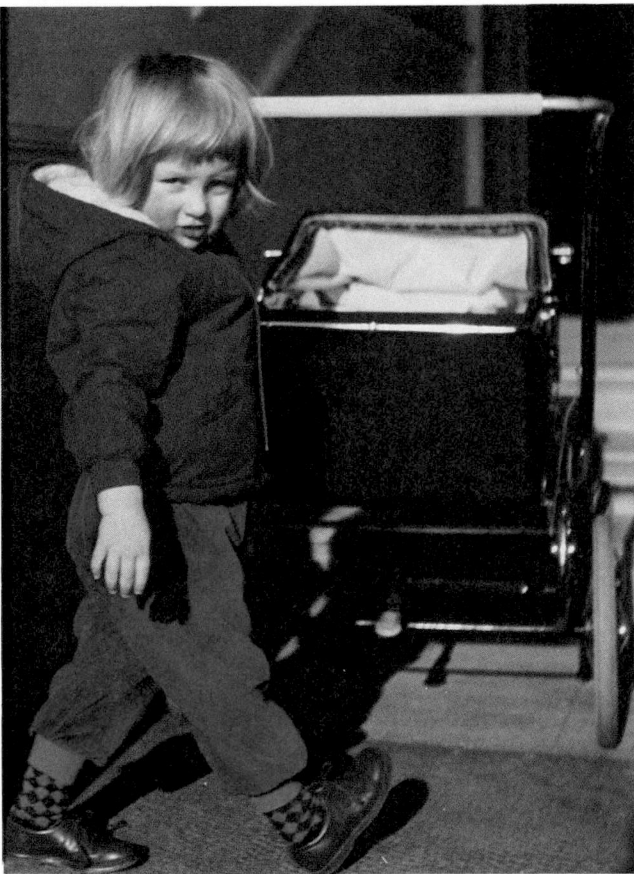

enchantment for the little girl, she was never in awe of them. Her father had been an equerry to a king and a queen, and all four of her grandparents, the Spencers and the Fermoys, as well as three great-aunts, were at one time or another in the personal service of Queen Elizabeth the Queen Mother. Both Lady Diana's grandmothers, as Ladies-in-Waiting of the Queen Mother, became in the process close friends. Lady Diana's maternal grandmother, Lady Fermoy, a Scot like the Queen Mother, is today still in attendance as a Woman of the Bedchamber.

Lady Diana, asked before her engagement if close proximity to the Royal Family would make her feel nervous, replied: 'No, of course not! Why should it?' She was indeed unusually accustomed to seeing and talking to royalty from the start, and to seeing them in informal, holiday situations. Her upbringing would naturally teach her the good manners necessary to cope with the protocol that mixing with royalty required. As her father said: 'The average family wouldn't know what hit them if their daughter married the future king . . . But some of my family go back to the Saxons – so that sort of thing's not a bit new to me . . . Diana had to marry somebody, and I've known and worked for the Queen since Diana was a baby.'

As a child, however, Lady Diana saw very little of her royal neighbours. She also saw little of her grandfather, the 7th Earl Spencer, who lived at Althorp Hall in Northamptonshire. The 7th Earl,

Lady Diana in 1968 with her brother Charles

Lady Diana and her brother on Bert the camel on her seventh birthday

Jack, was not too fond of his only son, Johnny, and she only visited the Spencers' ancestral home when her mother took her there. No Christmases were ever spent at Althorp; holidays were divided between Park House, summer trips and visits to friends. Lady Diana's main companions were her mother and Miss Allen, her older sisters, her baby brother and her school-friends. In 1968, when she was seven, she went to a day-school, Silfield School in King's Lynn, where she remained for two years.

In 1969, on her eighth birthday, 1 July, Prince Charles was invested as the Prince of Wales in Caernarvon Castle.

Already, however, an event had happened that would, if she had been older, have had more impact and meaning than it did: her parents separated in 1967. They were divorced two years later, Lady Althorp, having been named in 1968 in another divorce, that of Peter Shand Kydd and his wife, Janet. The custody of the children was disputed, but given to their father; and in 1969, soon after her own divorce, Lady Althorp married Mr Shand Kydd and went to live in Sussex.

Lady Diana continued to see her mother and was able to treat her mother's absence from home as one of those adult aberrations so inexplicable but acceptable by a child. An *au pair* was engaged at Park House to look after the children and life went on – at school and in the holidays – with weekends spent with neighbours and going to children's parties. At one, given for her seventh birthday by her father, he hired a camel called Bert to give the children rides. She revelled in charades and dressing-up and revealed a mischievous talent for mimicry.

Although she could be as serious and as shy as any little girl, she was also quite self-assertive, showing something of the strong, extrovert character of her mother – derived as it was from a rich blend of Scottish, Irish and American ancestors. Lady Diana, although said to be the first *English* bride of an heir apparent since Anne Hyde who married the future James II three hundred years ago – and likely to be the first English Queen Consort since Henry VIII's sixth wife, Katharine Parr – is in fact very *British*, and part American.

It was when she was eight or nine that she fell off a horse and broke her arm: it took over two months to mend. As a result she completely lost her riding nerve. 'I might take it up again,' she said recently. 'But very gently.'

She was ten when in 1971 she went – dressed in a dark red jacket and a grey pleated skirt and laden with a trunk labelled 'D. Spencer' – as a boarder to Riddlesworth Hall, a preparatory school near Diss in Norfolk. 'That was a dreadful day,' said her father. 'Dreadful losing her.' He did his best to satisfy her requests for tuck – chocolate cakes, ginger biscuits and Twiglets.

Lady Diana Spencer, at Itchenor, West Sussex, during the summer of 1970

The school's caring, family-like atmosphere in some way made up for the split in her family at home: her sisters, now teenagers, were very much involved in their own lives, and in 1972 her mother moved 500 miles away to the Scottish Isle of Seil, where she helped her husband run a hill-farm. The headmistress of Riddlesworth Hall was Miss Elizabeth Ridsdale – known as 'Riddy' – now retired; she had been headmistress for more than twenty years when Lady Diana became one of her pupils. Miss Ridsdale recalls: 'She was always a decent, kind and happy little girl. Everyone seemed to like her . . . She was good at games, especially swimming, which was very well taught at the school. She took part in everything . . . What stands out in my mind is how awfully sweet she was with the little ones.' The school, which allowed the girls to keep pets such as guinea-pigs and rabbits in hutches in the grounds, has a good

Overleaf: Lady Diana visited her mother in Scotland in her school holidays. She is seen here in 1974 with Soufflé, a Shetland pony.

academic reputation. Many pupils move on to Benenden School and Wycombe Abbey. Miss Ridsdale says of Lady Diana: 'She passed her Common Entrance to West Heath and did quite well in the exam.'

Lady Diana was a leggy twelve-year-old when in 1973 she went to West Heath, a small, tightly run school near Sevenoaks in Kent. In charge of the 130 pupils, whose day began at 7.30 a.m., was Miss Ruth Rudge, an Australian with firm but kindly views about education and the need for discipline. At the same time, the girls were allowed to 'develop their own minds and tastes and to realize their duties as citizens'. They were also encouraged to exert themselves in activities, not necessarily academic ones, that gave them confidence and character. Of Lady Diana, Miss Rudge said later: 'She's a girl who notices what needs to be done, then does it willingly and cheerfully.' As at her other schools, her academic achievements were not notable; her reports are said to have been 'normal and average'. Again, she is remembered for her 'cheerful personality' and 'willingness to help'. Lady Diana, now a tall, gawky girl with a fringe, was one of six girls sharing a dormitory, on whose wall was a colour photograph of the Prince of Wales in full regalia, taken at his investiture in 1969 at Caernarvon.

She learned to play the piano, but did not persevere. She was very keen on dancing, and learned ballet and tap-dancing at West Heath. Her ambition at one time was to be a dancer, and when she left school she continued for a while with her dancing lessons. 'I'm obsessed with ballet and I also love tap-dancing,' she has said. 'I always wanted to be a ballet dancer and started taking lessons when I was three and a half. But I just grew too tall.' She grew to be 5ft 10ins, the same height as her mother, whose strikingly attractive looks, long legs and swift stride have been inherited by her daughter, along with an open and positive approach to life and people.

But although Lady Diana did not become 'captain of everything' as her mother had been at school, she was captain of hockey and 'jolly keen at sport', her best endeavours being in swimming and diving, for which she won several school and inter-school cups. 'A' levels were not attempted. But when she left school in July 1977 – the summer of the Queen's Silver Jubilee year and soon after her sixteenth birthday – Lady Diana was given an award for service. Said Miss Rudge: 'We don't give this every year. It's presented only to outstanding pupils . . . I think Diana was surprised she had won it.'

While she was at West Heath, she used to visit an old lady once a week, helping her with the shopping and some domestic chores, and once a week she visited a centre for handicapped children, helping to do what she could. During the holidays she travelled to Scotland to be with her mother, with whom she is on very good terms. She had her own bedroom in the Shand Kydd house on the Isle of Seil, and took her school-friends there on holiday with her. It was an open-air life, tramping over the island and the mainland hills, fishing for mackerel, going out in her step-father's boat to put down lobster-pots, sailing on expeditions up and down the coast, and even swimming in the cold Atlantic. At night she sometimes watched television, unselectively, favouring the madcap humours of programmes like 'The Muppet Show' and 'Not the Nine o'Clock News'. Her collection of records expanded to include those with a strong melodic content such as discs by Abba and Neil Diamond; in classical music she preferred such composers as Tchaikovsky and Greig. In the winter there were parties and balls and Highland dancing. But in 1975 she stopped going home for half of each holiday to Park House. For in the summer her grandfather, the 7th Earl Spencer, died, and her father succeeded to the title as the 8th Earl. The family moved out of Park House to Althorp. No one has lived in Park House since then, and the birthplace of Lady Diana and her mother has stood empty for seven years.

The move in 1975 to Althorp – where her father remembers her 'flying down the front staircase on a tea-tray . . . playing "bears in the dark" in the portrait gallery' – was followed in 1976 by a more traumatic event, when the Countess of Dartmouth moved into Althorp, reorganized the running of the Spencers' family home and soon married the lonely 8th Earl, Diana's father.

He was named in the divorce proceedings brought against the Countess of Dartmouth by the Earl of Dartmouth, who as the Hon. Gerald Legge had been one of Earl Spencer's school-friends at Eton. As Gerald Legge he had married Raine McCorquodale, 'Deb of the Year' in 1947; her mother was the prolific, romantic novelist, Barbara Cartland. Like Lady Diana's mother, Raine McCorquodale was eighteen at the time of her marriage, and the groom, then aged twenty-four, was a captain in the Coldstream Guards. They became Lord and Lady Lewisham before he succeeded his uncle as the 9th Earl of Dartmouth; they were married for twenty-eight years. Two months after the Dartmouths were divorced, Earl Spencer and the dynamic 'do-gooding' Countess were married. None of the Earl's four children was informed in advance about the wedding and as a result none was able to attend the civil ceremony. Since when, an uneasy relationship has remained between the Earl's children and their step-mother, Lady Spencer, although it was slightly ameliorated in 1977 after their father had a brain haemorrhage and a

Lady Diana with her mother Mrs Peter Shand Kydd (above) and (right) introducing Lady Sarah Armstrong-Jones to the Earl and Countess Spencer at Lady Sarah Spencer's wedding in May 1980.

stroke. 'She saved my life,' he said later. She tended him for four months, nursing him, nudging and nagging him back to life. 'I love her dearly,' he says.

A year after Lady Diana's father remarried, another event occurred that would have a much greater impact on her life. In November 1977, while she was in her last term at West Heath, she went home to Althorp one weekend, a weekend when the Prince of Wales was the Spencers' guest on a shoot. Late on the Saturday morning, her eldest sister, Lady Sarah introduced Lady Diana to him. She was sixteen – he was nearly twenty-nine years old.

The following month she left West Heath – despite her father's advice to her to stay on and finish the school year. She had had enough of being a schoolgirl and had no wish to study for the doubtful reward of the odd 'A' level. A compromise was reached, and at her mother's suggestion Lady Diana went in January 1978 to an exclusive finishing school, the Institut Alpin Videmanette at Château d'Oex near Gstaad in Switzerland. Lady Sarah had also been to the Institut and much enjoyed herself there. Lady Diana took classes in domestic science, dress-making, cooking, both French and Swiss dishes, and a typing and correspondence course. She improved on her 'O' level French and she learned to ski. On Saturday evenings the girls, escorted by chaperones, were allowed into Gstaad for a glimpse of the night-life. But the school's aim was to make its sixty charges 'healthy and happy by ensuring they work hard and play hard in a relaxed family atmosphere.' They had very little free time. This continuance of a jolly 'all-girls-together' regime – and few of the girls were English – was not quite to Lady Diana's liking: she began to feel that something was missing, something more positive. Her French teacher said: 'We discussed life in general and what the girls wanted to do. Lady Diana was broad-minded, but she was also very idealistic about what she wanted for herself. She knew she wanted to work with children – and then she wanted to get married and have children of her own.' Before long she would achieve the first two of those aims.

She was perhaps also unsettled in February by the presence of Lady Sarah at Klosters on a skiing holiday in the company of Prince Charles. Although Klosters was at the other end of Switzerland, near the Austrian border, Lady Diana could not have ignored the excited chatter and speculation of the girls about her sister's 'romance' with the Prince of Wales. The school's headmistress, Madame Yersin, has said: 'When Lady Diana arrived she was a lovely girl – but rather young for a sixteen-year-old – and while she was a pretty girl, she was not the beauty she's blossomed into now. We've heard that she was secretly in love with Prince Charles. If so, the publicity about Lady Sarah must have been hard on her. Things like that are very difficult for a girl of that age to cope with.'

For whatever reason, Lady Diana was only at the Institut for one term, somewhat to Madame Yersin's surprise. 'Most of our pupils stay for a year and sit our exams,' she said. 'Lady Diana did not come back to sit her exams and we were not told why.' Her mother's explanation for her daughter's departure was that she did not want to spend the summer 'just picking flowers'. She also wanted to be in England for the twenty-first birthday of her sister, Lady Jane, to whom she was particularly close, and for Lady Jane's forthcoming marriage to the Queen's assistant private secretary, Robert Fellowes, in April 1978.

When she returned to London in March 1978, Lady Diana moved for a time into her mother's flat in Cadogan Place, which she shared with a friend, Sophie Kimball; there was room for a third girl, but the third flatmate constantly changed. Shunning the debutante set since she had no wish to 'come out', Lady Diana began looking after children, as she had always wanted to do, offering her services to married friends as an unpaid nanny and children's help.

For over a year, from April 1978 to July 1979, she cared for other people's babies and children, in particular for a two-year-old boy, Patrick, son of an American couple. She sat and talked to him for hours, invented games for him to play and took him on outings in his push-chair.

Soon after her seventeenth birthday, in July 1978, she passed her driving-test, on the first attempt, in Sevenoaks, Kent. But it was not until 1979 that she acquired a Volkswagen, which she crashed, and then a red Mini-Metro. For most of the time in London she rode around on a bicycle, until the attentions of the press prevented her from doing so.

For three months, in the autumn of 1978, she attended a Cordon Bleu cookery course run by Elizabeth Russell in Wimbledon. At weekends she went home to Althorp, staying on the estate in a farmhouse used by Lady Jane; usually she invited some girl-friends to join her. Most of her holidays were spent in Scotland; she also went skiing. Although she went to several charity dances, she did not enjoy the noisy, smoke-filled atmosphere of discothèques – she neither smokes nor drinks – nor the artificial pleasures of night-clubs. Her preference was for small dinner-parties with friends in her flat or in a favoured restaurant, for a game of bridge, for visits to the cinema or theatre. But in the spring of 1979, she decided to get a regular job, at a nursery school, the Young England Kindergarten in Pimlico, and as a practical symbol of her growing independence, her parents bought her an unfurnished flat in South Kensington.

The three-bedroomed flat (in Coleherne Court, a four-storey mansion-block on the corner of Old Brompton Road) cost her mother and father £50,000. In July 1979 Lady Diana moved in, furnishing the flat in a warm but simple Habitat style and repainting its white walls in a variety of pastel colours, assisted by some friends: the sitting-room walls became pale primrose yellow while the bathroom wallpaper was bright with red cherries. An upright piano was acquired when a former school-friend from West Heath, Carolyn Pride, who was studying music, came to share the flat. By August she had been joined by Anne Bolton and Virginia Pitman. In September, Lady Diana went to work at the kindergarten which was in a Pimlico church hall.

It was run by Mrs Victoria Wilson, and Kay Seth-Smith who had been to West Heath. Lady Diana much enjoyed her year-and-a-half at the school, watching over the fifty or so under-fives who were left there daily by their mothers or nannies, and among whom were the offspring of wealthier bankers, lawyers, politicians and actors. She taught the children drawing, painting and dancing and joined in the games she and they devised. Although she never had

Coleherne Court: Lady Diana shared a flat here until she became engaged to Prince Charles.

any formal training in child-care, she was a 'natural' – 'a pied-piper with children,' according to her mother. She gave serious consideration to each child, treating them as small individuals, showing a genuine interest in what they were doing or trying to say and ready to help them when required to do so. Misbehaviour and tantrums were met with a firm word, a reproving glance, as often as not followed by a reassuring smile or a giggle – reminiscent of the kind of merriment shown both by her mother and her grandmother, Lady Fermoy. At the end of each morning she would help to tidy up, wash up mugs, and stow toys away, before bicycling back to Coleherne Court.

In the flat there was also much merriment as the four girls, in between answering the telephone, exchanged news and views. In their wardrobes the variety of their interests was reflected by the variety of clothes: Lady Diana's choice ranged from corduroy culottes, Fiorucci sweat-shirts, a borrowed corduroy smoking jacket, to lambswool pullovers from Benneton, cardigans from Friends, cotton shirts and skirts from Laura Ashley, and suits and evening dresses from Harrods and Emanuel. Her jewelry was discreet: simple earrings and pendants, a string of pearls; some gifts from her mother. In the hall which was partly blocked by bicycles, theatre programmes mainly from Covent Garden, piled up on a chest; on the sitting-room coffee-table, among the fashion and women's magazines, were copies of *Private Eye*. There was always much activity: dinners, parties, shows, the cinema, visits by or to friends; and then there were the weekends in the country, with journeys by car or train to Althorp and also to stay with friends at other country-houses – and an invitation to Balmoral.

In August 1979 she went to Balmoral to join the royal house-party as a guest of the Queen and as a companion for Prince Andrew. She was just eighteen, he was nineteen. It might have seemed to the older women of both families that the handsome young man and the beautiful girl made a fine match. But there was never any romance – they enjoyed each other's company and remained good friends.

In February 1980 she was invited to Sandringham, again as a companion for Prince Andrew. She travelled to Norfolk with Amanda Knatchbull, grand-daughter of Earl Mountbatten, and further improved the good impression the older members of the Royal Family, who had known her since she was a little girl, already had of her. She was fondly and favourably regarded; but the Prince of Wales, who was also there, saw little of her, being surrounded by his own group of friends.

Then came the three royal invitations that would change her life. In July, she was asked by Prince Charles if she would like to watch a polo match one Saturday in Sussex. He was playing for *Les Diables Bleus*. A week or so later, she was asked by Prince Philip if she would like to join the Royal Family on board the Royal Yacht, *Britannia*, during Cowes Week (the first week in August). Later that month she was invited by the Queen to Balmoral for the first week of September, during the Highland Games at Braemar. She never saw the Games; she saw much of Prince Charles, and a newspaper photographer snapped her watching the Prince fishing for salmon in the River Dee.

It was the last weekend of her anonymity and of nineteen years of privacy. On Monday, 8 September, her name and photograph appeared for the first time in the national tabloids. She was headline news and remained so for five extraordinary months, braving the ordeal of trial by the press as she tried to carry on a normal existence while being courted by the Prince of Wales. Despite pressures that would have made a film-star scream, she never faltered, being as patient, considerate, amused and as sensible with the press as she was with a child. She behaved impeccably, winning the respect even of those who harassed her, and above all the far greater respect of the Royal Family and the Prince of Wales.

The Royal Yacht 'Britannia' at Cowes in 1980

If the Queen or Prince Philip had been asked during the last ten years about the kind of girl they hoped their eldest son would marry one day, most probably they would have described someone with the qualities and nature of Lady Diana. She has grace, beauty, charm and tact; she is kind, loyal, good-humoured, good-natured, strong-minded and well-bred; she has vitality and youth; she is descended from kings, and her family has faithfully served royalty for centuries. She will be a good wife, a good mother, and a good friend, giving the Prince of Wales the wholehearted love and respect he will need and rely on in the years ahead – which he will treasure and return.

Left: Prince Andrew – Lady Diana was often his companion before her relationship with Prince Charles.

CHAPTER 3

The Family of the Bride

It seems inconceivable now that Prince Charles could ever have married anyone else. Not only was Lady Diana 'The Girl Next Door' and a 'Girl Without a Past', her ancestral past added lustre to her title of 'The Most Suitable Girl'. For blood and breeding matter in the best families, to whom succession is nine points of the law of property, and although some say kind hearts are worth more than coronets, and simple faith than Norman blood, when kind hearts, coronets, simple faith and Norman blood are all conjoined, then must the parents of a prince have four-fold reason to rejoice.

Lady Diana's pedigree must have pleased the Palace. Despite its bends sinister, they at least were royal. In fact the ancestry of the House of Spencer is a good deal more regular than that of the House of Windsor.

The bride and groom are eleventh cousins, once removed, from James I, or – put another way – they are sixteenth cousins, once removed, with a common ancestor in Henry VII. They are also seventh cousins, once removed, via William Cavendish, the 3rd Duke of Devonshire (1698–1755). Their main and manifold links were forged through Charles II and his brother James II: five lines of descent being traced through King Charles's many assorted offspring and one through an illegitimate daughter of James II and Arabella Churchill, the daughter of the original Sir Winston Churchill (1620–88) and sister of the 1st Duke of Marlborough.

The known illegitimate progeny of Charles II numbered thirteen, variously produced by seven of his mistresses: Lucy Walter, Elizabeth Killigrew, Catherine Pegge, Barbara Villiers (mother of five of his children), Nell Gwynn, Moll Davis, and Louise de Kéroüalle.

The first of these, Lucy Walter, a Welsh girl, captivated the teenage Prince Charles in 1648 in The Hague, where the women and children of many Royalist families during the Civil War had sought refuge. They were both eighteen at the time. She was the daughter of William Walter of Roche Castle near Haverfordwest in Pembrokeshire and a niece of the 1st Earl of Carbery. The family went to Holland after the castle was destroyed by Cromwell's Parliamentary troops in 1644. The diarist, John Evelyn, who met her in 1649, described her as 'a brown, beautiful, bold but insipid creature', and it was in April 1649, three months after the execution of Charles I, that she gave birth in Rotterdam to a son, named James

Left: Charles II, 1685, by Sir Godfrey Kneller. The King is one of the royal ancestors shared by Lady Diana and Prince Charles.

Right: Lucy Walter, one of Charles II's mistresses, by Antoine Palamedes. Lady Lavinia Bingham, a descendant of their daughter Mary Sarsfield, married the 2nd Earl Spencer.

Barbara Villiers, Lady Castlemaine (1641–1709), by Sir Peter Lely (1618–80). She was another of Charles II's mistresses. Adelaide Horatia Seymour, a descendant of their son Henry, married the 4th Earl Spencer.

Crofts after William Crofts, one of Queen Henrietta's attendants in the Royal Family's exile. The father, however, was young Prince Charles, who later officially acknowledged his first son and ennobled him as the Duke of Monmouth in 1663.

Lucy accompanied the exiled Prince of Wales on his travels for a few years and produced another child, Mary, in May 1651. The previous year, during his abortive expedition to Scotland, she had formed an association with Colonel Bennet, later Earl of Arlington – in fact some said he was Mary's father – and thus probably incurred the royal displeasure. Prince Charles abandoned her, and she abandoned herself to 'a life of depravity'.

Her daughter, Mary, married William Sarsfield, and it is as Mrs Sarsfield that she enters the Spencer family tree. One of her descendants, Charles Bingham, became the 1st Earl of Lucan (1735–99), whose daughter, Lady Lavinia Bingham, became the wife of the 2nd Earl Spencer (1758–1834).

Another of Charles II's mistresses, whose plenty owed something to the fact that his wife, the Portuguese princess, Catherine of Braganza, was plain and childless, was Barbara Villiers, said to be the lewdest and loveliest of the King's concubines. Daughter of the 2nd Viscount Grandison, she married a certain Robert Palmer in 1659 when she was eighteen. Mrs Palmer produced a daughter Anne – whom the King acknowledged as his, although the Earl of Chesterfield was also said to be the father – in February 1661, and Mr Palmer was created the 1st Earl of Castlemaine in December. He did not, it appears, father any of his wife's children.

Her next child to be sired by Charles II was a son, Charles, later ennobled as the 1st Duke of Cleveland, who was born in June 1662, less than a month after the King's marriage to Catherine of Braganza. Lady Castlemaine in due course became a Woman of the Queen's Bedchamber. Her own bedchamber was often visited by the King – on an average four evenings a week, according to Samuel Pepys. Her third child, another boy, was born in September 1663. Called Henry, he became the 1st Duke of Grafton, one of whose descendants, Adelaide Horatia Seymour, married the 4th Earl Spencer (1798–1857).

Lady Castlemaine had two more children by the King, in 1664 and 1665, and was created Duchess of Cleveland in 1670, in consideration of her noble descent and of 'her own personal virtues'. An avaricious but extravagant woman with a lust for intrigue and an intriguing list of lovers – including a rope-dancer, the playwright, William Wycherley, and John Churchill (later Duke of Marlborough) – the Duchess of Cleveland became one of the wealthiest women in London and the most notorious. Her last child – the father this time was an actor – was born in 1686, when the Duchess was forty-five. King Charles had died the year before. The Duchess died in 1709, of dropsy, which 'swelled her gradually to a monstrous bulk'.

Another descendant of Mrs Mary Sarsfield, daughter of Lucy Walter, was Lady Diana's paternal grandmother, Lady Cynthia, wife of the 7th Earl Spencer, who was known as Jack. Through Lady Cynthia, two lines of descent can be traced back via the Lucan and Abercorn families to the 1st Duke of Richmond, the last, acknowledged illegitimate son of Charles II by his French mistress, Louise de Kéroüalle. She became one of Queen Catherine's maids of honour in 1670, when she was twenty-one, and one of the King's mistresses the following year. Their son, the future Duke of Richmond, duly appeared nine months later and in 1673 she became a Lady of the Bedchamber and Duchess of Portsmouth. John Evelyn said she had 'a childish, simple and baby face'; King Charles, because she was chubby, called her 'Fubbs'; and Nell Gwynn referred to her as 'Squintabella' and 'Weeping Willow' because of the Duchess of Portsmouth's almond-shaped eyes and tendency to weep at will. As the Duchess was French and a Catholic she was much disliked by Protestant

Louise de Kéroüalle, Duchess of Portsmouth (1644–1734), by Philippe Mignard, 1622. The 1st Duke of Richmond, son of Charles II and Louise de Kéroüalle, is an ancestor of Lady Diana.

Londoners and denigrated in a scurrilous ballad of the day as 'Portsmouth, the incestuous Punk'. Sir John Reresby described her as 'the most absolute of all the King's mistresses'. She was also, thanks to her cossetting of the King, the cosy luxury of her apartments in Whitehall and her French cuisine, the most enduring. Although barred from his bedchamber when Charles II lay dying, she remained near him, stricken with grief but sufficiently concerned to impress upon the King's brother, the Catholic Duke of York (soon to be James II), that the King himself was a secret member of the Church of Rome and must receive that Church's final blessings and consolation. So it was that the day before he died, Charles II confessed his sins, somewhat briefly, and was given the communion and extreme unction by a Scottish Roman Catholic priest called Hudleston.

Apart from Lady Diana's connection with the Earls of Lucan through the Duke of Richmond, son of Louise de Kéroüalle, there is a link between the Lucans and her mother's second husband, Peter Shand Kydd. Christina, the wife of his half-brother, former champion amateur jockey, William Shand Kydd, is the sister of Veronica Moorhouse Duncan, who in 1963 married the 7th Earl of Lucan, missing since November 1974 after the murder of his children's nanny.

Another interesting ancestress of the Spencers was Charlot, Countess of Schomberg (1659–96), who provides a further royal connection. She was the

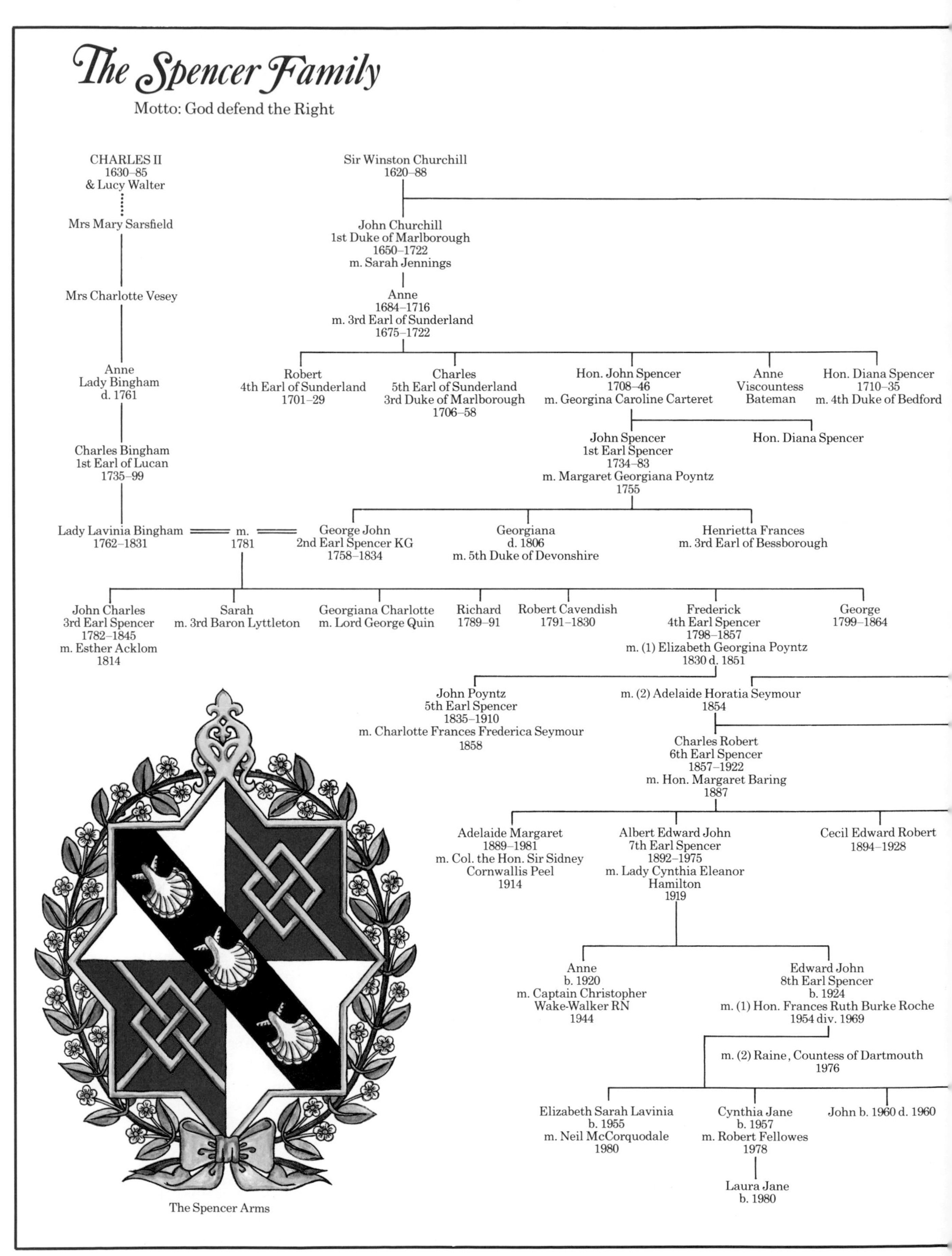

The Spencer Arms

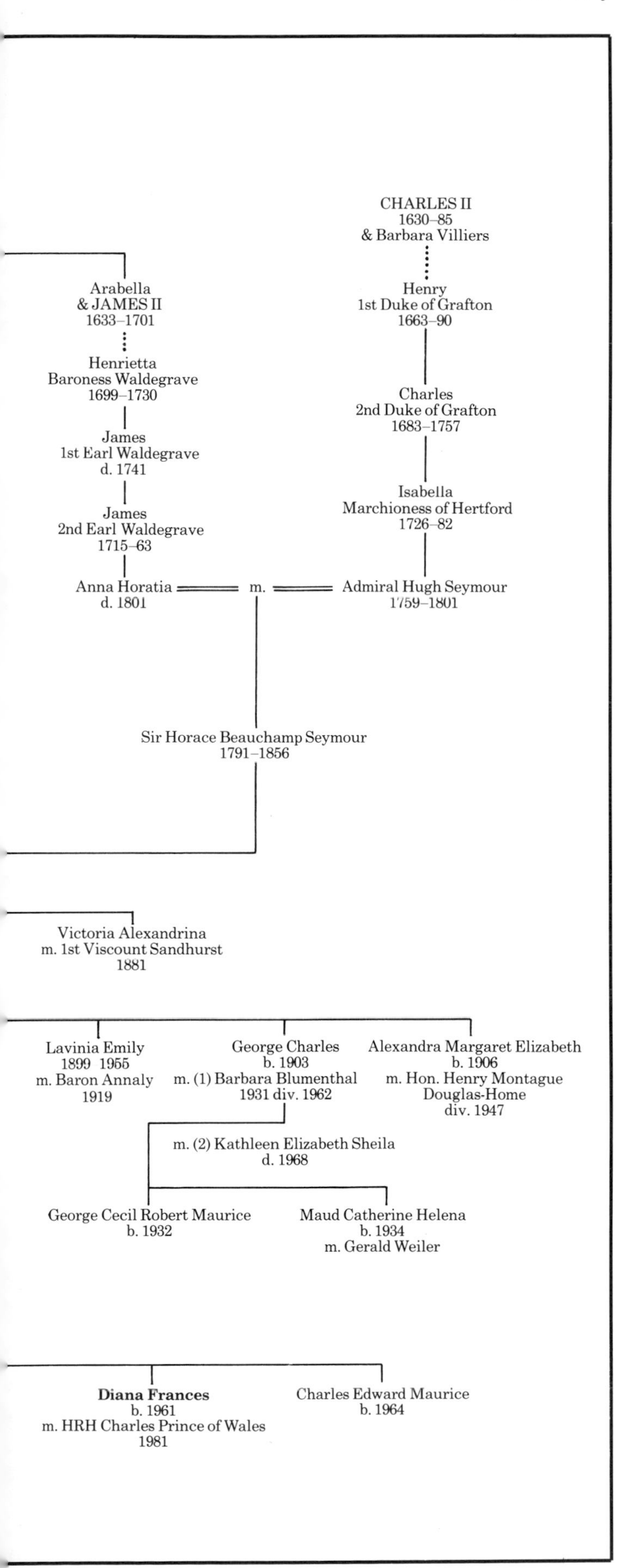

illegitimate daughter of the Elector Palatine, Charles Louis (1617–80), and grand-daughter of Frederick V, who in 1613 married Princess Elizabeth, the daughter of James I. This Elizabeth, the sister of the future Charles I, eventually became the aunt of Charles II and James II. She was also (after her marriage to Frederick V, the Elector Palatine) the mother of Sophia, who in turn married the Elector of Hanover, Ernest Augustus. It was their son, George, who became George I in 1714 on the death of the last of the crowned Stuarts, Queen Anne.

Genealogical comparisons, generally so odious to others, may well amuse the Prince and Princess of Wales some idle evening at Highgrove when, with their respective pedigrees spread out before them, they might pick out threads of relative interest and discover how they are connected.

The Spencers and Althorp

Genealogy becomes more lively when the bare bones of familial fact are vivified by the flesh and blood of family history. The Spencers can trace their family back to the Norman-French adherents of William the Conqueror, who acquired land and authority at the expense of the English. For centuries the Spencers have been loyal and attentive servants of the Crown, their original wealth and status increasing with the land they acquired. Sheep were the basis of their fortune, with careful management, modest aspirations, luck, and the thoughtful selection of heiresses as brides.

The present 8,488-acre Althorp estate in Northamptonshire was originally leased from the Abbot of Evesham in 1486 by John Spencer, a Warwickshire farmer and landowner who lived in Wormleighton Manor. His nephew and heir, Sir John Spencer (knighted in 1511 by Henry VIII), bought the land and the moated, red-brick house with its central courtyard in 1506. It was his grandson, another Sir John, a Lord Mayor of London, who in 1573 added the forecourt wings, although the Spencer's main residence continued to be Wormleighton Manor. Two generations later, Sir Robert Spencer, possessor at the age of thirty-three of 19,000 sheep and reputedly of more ready money than anyone else in England, was in 1603 created Baron Spencer of Wormleighton on the accession of James I. In the same year, King James's consort, Queen Anne, stopped at Althorp (pronounced 'Alltrup') on her way from Edinburgh to join her husband in London. With her was her eldest son, Henry, soon to be created Prince of Wales – he was invested in 1610. They stayed a night at Althorp, after seeing a masque written by Ben Jonson in honour of their visit.

William, the 2nd Baron Spencer, who was born at Althorp in 1591, married Lady Penelope Wriothesley,

Left: Earl and Countess Spencer outside Althorp House

Right: Robert Spencer, 2nd Earl of Sunderland (1640–1702), by Sir Peter Lely. He furnished Althorp with paintings and furniture from his European travels.

Below: Althorp in 1677, by Sir John Vorsterman. Robert Spencer, 2nd Earl of Sunderland, employed an Italian architect to remodel the house, and the Frenchman Le Nôtre to improve the gardens.

daughter of Shakespeare's friend and patron the Earl of Southampton. They had six sons and four daughters. The 2nd Baron was an enthusiastic horseman, and apart from building a racecourse on the estate, he established the Easter race-meetings on nearby Harlestone Heath.

His eldest son, Henry, born in 1620, had a brief but crowded life. He became the 3rd Baron Spencer at the age of sixteen, the same year that he went to Magdalen College in Oxford. He travelled in France, married Lady Dorothy Sidney (the 'Sacharissa' of Edmund Waller's poems) in 1639, when he was nineteen, and a few years later became Lord Lieutenant of Northamptonshire. When King Charles I raised his standard at Nottingham in August 1642 at the start of the Civil War, Henry, Lord Spencer, an ardent Royalist, financed the King's cause with a loan of £10,000. In return he was rewarded with an earldom, that of Sunderland, in June 1643. But a few months later, at the Battle of Newbury, the new earl was killed – he was twenty-three. Three years later, after Prince Rupert had stayed overnight at Wormleighton, the old family home was burned down by Royalist forces, to prevent the Manor being used as a garrison by rebel Parliamentarian troops.

However, the family's fortunes and possessions survived Cromwell's Commonwealth. The young Earl's widow was able in 1650 to enclose the courtyard, turning it into a grand hall with a gallery and great staircase; and the four children her young husband had fathered before he died prospered.

Their eldest son, Robert, the 2nd Earl of Sunderland, was born in Paris and became a brilliant politician, a great schemer and a man of few scruples, who made himself indispensable to three kings: Charles II, James II and William III. In his time he became Ambassador to Paris, Cologne and Madrid, Secretary of State, Lord President of the Council, Lord Chamberlain and the first Spencer Knight of the Garter. He also patronized the arts, collecting paintings and furniture, much of it on his European travels. He embellished Althorp with his acquisitions, so that the rooms, according to John Evelyn, were 'such as may become a prince'. Lely's portraits of the Hampton Court Beauties, hung in a special carved frame named after the Earl and called a Sunderland, were displayed in the 115-foot-long Picture Gallery, where ladies walked for exercise when the weather was bad. Several Van Dycks and works by famous Dutch and Italian artists also adorned the walls. An Italian architect was employed by the 2nd Earl to remodel the house, inside and out, and a Frenchman, Le Nôtre, who had designed the gardens at Versailles, was brought to Althorp to improve the park. The elm avenues he

designed, decimated in the 1970s by Dutch elm disease, have recently been replanted by the 8th Earl Spencer.

Charles, the 3rd Earl of Sunderland (1675–1722), was a Whig politician of uncertain temperament and affiliations, who eventually became, like his father, Lord President of the Council and then First Lord of the Treasury in the reign of George I. He collected books and had three wives. The second, Lady Anne Churchill, was a daughter of the 1st Duke of Marlborough, the victor at Blenheim. She produced five children, three of whom were boys. They became in turn: the 4th Earl of Sunderland, who died unmarried when he was twenty-eight; Charles, the 5th Earl, who by special patent succeeded to the title of 3rd Duke of Marlborough as the 1st Duke left no male heirs; and the Hon. John Spencer, who took over Althorp in 1734 when his older brother, Charles, moved into Blenheim Palace. Althorp was in the process of being remodelled once again, and the entrance hall, whose walls were being covered by the horse and hunting paintings of John Wootton, was adorned with a ducal coronet above the door.

The Hon. John Spencer, the favourite grandson of Sarah Jennings, Dowager Duchess of Marlborough, was also her principal beneficiary when she died. She left him a fortune in money, horses, property, paintings and china. Through her, his youngest sister, Lady Diana Spencer, almost became Princess of Wales. For the ever-ambitious Dowager Duchess of Marlborough had also doted on her, and had planned in 1735 to marry Lady Diana to Frederick, eldest son of George II and as such the Prince of Wales. The Dowager Duchess was prepared to provide Lady Diana with a huge dowry, £100,000, which the Prince of Wales needed to pay off his debts. Preparations for a wedding in the Dowager Duchess's house in Windsor Great Park were secretly made. But the Prime Minister, Sir Robert Walpole, heard of the proposed union and intervened. He had other ideas for the Prince of Wales's bride. So had George II – and in April 1736, Prince Frederick married the seventeen-year-old Princess Augusta of Saxe-Gotha in St James's Palace. Lady Diana became Duchess of Bedford instead.

A second Diana, the Hon. John Spencer's only daughter, never married.

John Spencer died in 1746 when he was thirty-eight. His death occurred, according to Horace Walpole 'because he would not be abridged of those invaluable blessings of an English subject, brandy, small-beer and tobacco'. His only son, John (1734–83),

The Hon. John Spencer (1708–46) with his son John, afterwards 1st Earl Spencer (1734–83), and the page, Caesar Shaw, by George Knapton

Georgiana, Countess Spencer (1737–1814) and her eldest daughter Lady Georgiana Spencer, afterwards Duchess of Devonshire (1757–1806), by Sir Joshua Reynolds

after being created Baron Spencer of Althorp and Viscount Spencer by George III in 1761, became *the 1st Earl Spencer* in 1765. He was MP for Warwick, High Steward of St Albans, and also a patron of the arts, his friends including the painter, Sir Joshua Reynolds, David Garrick the actor, and the leading Whig, Charles James Fox. He built Spencer House, overlooking Green Park (now offices), in London. His marriage in 1755, when he was twenty-one, to Georgiana Poyntz, was performed secretly in his mother's dressing-room (now the Oak Room) at Althorp during a ball attended by 500 guests. They had three children, the last two being girls, both of whom also nearly married a Prince of Wales – like their great-aunt Lady Diana.

The elder girl, Georgiana, although wedded to the 5th Duke of Devonshire, went as far as bedding the portly Prince of Wales, who would later be George IV. She was known as 'the Duchess of Dimples' and 'the face without a frown'. She married the Duke when she was seventeen, but was mistress to more than one man. When she became pregnant in 1785 it was not known whether the father was the Duke or the Prince of Wales.

Twenty-four years later, her younger sister, Henrietta, wife of the Earl of Bessborough, almost became another of the Prince of Wales's mistresses. She described one of the Prince's propositions to her in a letter to a former lover, Lord Granville, in 1809 when she was forty-eight: 'He threw himself on his knees, and clasping me round, kissed my neck before I was aware . . . He continued, sometimes struggling with me, sometimes sobbing and crying . . . Vows of eternal love, entreaties, promises of what he would do – he would break with Mrs Fitzherbert and Lady Hertford – I should *make my own terms*!!'

He did not win her, and so a second Spencer lady failed to be wedded and bedded by a Prince of Wales.

Regardless of the irregular royal connections of the 1st Earl's two daughters (or because of them), further distinctions were gained by their brother, George, *the 2nd Earl Spencer* (1758–1834), who became Ambassador to Vienna, Lord Privy Seal under William Pitt, First Lord of the Admiralty, and Secretary of State. He was also Master of Trinity House and an avid book-collector: his library of 40,000 early books and manuscripts – fifty-eight printed by Caxton – was said to be the finest in Europe. He also invented a new style of waistcoat, known as a Spencer.

On succeeding to the title in 1783, he commissioned the architect who had designed Brook's Club, Carlton House and Brighton Pavilion, Henry Holland, to renovate and restore Althorp and its gardens, giving them their present appearance. Holland filled in the moat and refaced the house with cream-coloured tiles made at Ipswich. Some corridors were added, rooms were refurnished and redecorated, and the state rooms were moved from the first floor to the ground floor, those in the west wing becoming the Dining Room (now the South Drawing Room), the Yellow Drawing Room and the Long Library. Further alterations were made to the house around 1870 and again in 1947 and 1977.

The 3rd Earl Spencer, John Charles (1782–1845), educated at Harrow when Byron was there, married Esther Acklom in 1814. The marriage 'was not of his own seeking', according to the *Farington Diary*, and was made to comply with his parents' wishes, and 'since Jack Althorp would not propose to her, she proposed to him; and such an unusual proceeding was fraught with happy consequences . . . His devotion after marriage amply compensated for his lack of ardour before.' Esther Acklom, 'although stout and somewhat plain in appearance', was 'a decided flirt'. She was also an heiress.

When she died in childbirth four years later, aged twenty-nine, the widowed and childless Earl devoted himself to politics and farming. He was MP for Northamptonshire and South Northamptonshire, Leader of the House of Commons under Lord Gray, Fellow of the Royal Society, a Privy Councillor and Chancellor of the Exchequer. He founded and became the first President of the Royal Agricultural Society and had a hand in the establishment of the Royal Agricultural College at Cirencester in Gloucestershire. He bred Shorthorn cattle and was Master of the Pytchley Hunt.

After his death Lord Greville wrote: 'No man ever died with a fairer character, or more generally regretted . . . He was the very model and type of an English gentleman . . . modest without diffidence, confident without vanity, ardently desiring the good of his country, without the slightest personal ambition . . . He exercised in the House of Commons an influence and even a dominion greater than any leader either after or before him . . . It was impossible for anyone . . . not to respect him. Nothing could make him lose his temper. In the greatest scenes of uproar and confusion . . . there he stood, motionless as a statue – his face shadowing forth the most perfect placidness of mind.'

The title passed in 1845 to his younger brother, Frederick, *the 4th Earl Spencer* (1798–1857) who was then forty-eight. He joined the Royal Navy when he was thirteen and served on board the *Royal George*, *Blake* and *Malta* as a midshipman during the Napoleonic Wars. Promoted Lieutenant in 1818 when on the *Glasgow*, he became captain of the *Talbot* in 1825 and fought at the Battle of Navarino. For ten years a Whig MP, he then became Equerry to the Duchess of Kent, a Privy Councillor, Lord Chamberlain, Rear Admiral and Vice Admiral, and lastly Lord Steward of the Household. His first wife and second cousin, Elizabeth Georgina Poyntz, died in 1851; he remarried three years later, his second wife being Adelaide Seymour.

His only son by his first wife became *the 5th Earl*. John Poyntz (1835–1910), known as the Red Earl because of his bushy beard of that hue, was educated at Harrow and Cambridge where he studied law. His marriage in 1858 to Charlotte Seymour – 'Spenser's Faerie Queene' as she was called because of her beauty – produced no children. Briefly Liberal MP for South Northamptonshire in 1857, he was Groom of the Stole to the Prince Consort for two years and to the Prince of Wales (later Edward VII) for four, after which he became a Doctor of Civil Law at Oxford and a Doctor of Laws at Cambridge. He was Viceroy of Ireland twice, Lord Lieutenant of Northamptonshire (1872–1908), Lord President of the Council, First Lord of the Admiralty, Privy Seal to the Prince of Wales (1901–7) and a member of the Council of the Duchy of Cornwall. A keen sportsman and fox-hunter, he was

John Poyntz, 5th Earl Spencer (1835–1910), by F. Sergeant (1871). He was known as the Red Earl because of his red beard.

John, 7th Earl Spencer (1892–1975), by Augustus John. He was Lady Diana's grandfather.

thrice Master of the Pytchley Hunt. Lord Ribblesdale described him as being 'by nature obstinate and inflexible . . . With all his great qualities of industry, devotion to the public service and personal integrity, Lord Spencer was wanting in . . . "vision"'.

In 1883 the Spencers owned over 27,000 acres of England, said to bring in over £46,500 a year. Of this land 16,800 acres were in Northamptonshire, the rest being scattered about Warwickshire, Hertfordshire, Norfolk, Buckinghamshire, and Leicestershire, with two acres in Surrey. By 1981, owing to high death duties and the expensive upkeep of Althorp, more than half the estate had been sold. The present Earl now owns a total of 13,317 acres, of which 8,488 are the Althorp estate.

On the 5th Earl's death in 1910, his half brother, Charles, became *the 6th Earl* at the age of fifty-three. Thrice MP for North Northamptonshire, he was also Lord Lieutenant of the county, Vice Chamberlain and Lord Chamberlain (1905–12). His marriage to the Hon. Margaret Baring in 1887 produced six children. Their second son, Cecil, who was a lieutenant-commander in the Royal Navy during World War I and was awarded the *Croix de Guerre*, a Distinguished Service Cross and Bar, died as the result of a riding accident.

The first son, Albert John (1892–1975), and known as Jack, became *the 7th Earl Spencer* in 1922. He was Lady Diana's grandfather. He was educated at Harrow and Trinity College, Cambridge; he became a captain in the First Life Guards and served throughout World War I, in which he was badly wounded. After the war he devoted himself to the management and improvement of Althorp, taking a special interest, as Trustee of the Wallace Collection, in his own collection of priceless pictures. His hobby was tapestry, and several chairs at Althorp are backed with his work.

His sister, Lady Delia Peel, who died in 1981, was Extra Woman of the Bedchamber to Queen Elizabeth the Queen Mother; another sister, Lady Lavinia, and his wife, Lady Cynthia, also at one time served the Queen Mother as, respectively, Extra Lady-in-Waiting and Lady of the Bedchamber.

The 7th Earl married Lady Cynthia Hamilton, daughter of the 3rd Duke of Abercorn, in 1919. They had two children: Anne, who became a third officer in the WRNS in World War II and married Captain Christopher Wake-Walker RN in 1944, and Edward John, the present Earl and Lady Diana's father.

The 8th Earl Spencer was born in 1924. He went to Eton and Sandhurst, and became a captain in the Royal Scots Greys, after which he attended a course at the Royal Agricultural College in Cirencester. He is now Deputy Honorary Colonel of the Royal Anglian Regiment (Northants). He was ADC to the

Viscount Althorp, the present Earl Spencer, on his twenty-first birthday, 24 January 1945. Painting by Rodrigo Moynihan

Viscount Althorp (in the centre), as Equerry to the Queen, attended an investiture in New Zealand in 1954 when Sir William Goodfellow was knighted.

Governor of South Australia after World War II, and then became Equerry to George VI in 1950, when he was twenty-six. Two years later, on the death of King George, he was appointed Equerry to Queen Elizabeth II and accompanied her and Prince Philip on their first Commonwealth tour. He is Chairman of the National Association of Boys' Clubs, patron of twelve livings, and has been a member of Northamptonshire County Council for twenty years.

His second wife, Raine, has carefully improved the appearance of Althorp, inside and out, with many imaginative touches. She has also written the guidebook – the house is open to the public on Tuesday, Thursday and Saturday afternoons from April to October – and she says in it, with some pride and justification: 'Althorp . . . remains as a testimonial to all those Spencers who not only gave their time and energies in public service, but managed to add their own special contribution to the house.' The works of art of every kind acquired by the Spencers, she says, 'combine to give an overall impression of beauty and grandeur, yet retaining the intimacy and charm which can only be found where a family have cared for a house for hundreds of years and made it their home.'

The house, with its wonderful variety of pictures and furniture – it still contains one of the finest private art collections in Europe, including pictures by Titian, Holbein, Rubens, Van Dyck, Lely, Reynolds, Gainsborough, Kneller, Nicholson, Sargent and John – is indeed a delight and still a home fit to receive a prince. Prince Charles has stayed there on shooting weekends more than once, sleeping in King William's Room, in a four-poster bed occupied by King William of Orange in 1695. Lady Spencer is clearly not without a sense of humour: on a table in the room are some carefully arranged books, topped by a well-read paperback, *A Nightingale Sang* by Barbara Cartland.

Earl Spencer's first wife, whom he married (when he was Viscount Althorp) in June 1954, was the Hon. Frances Ruth Burke Roche, daughter of the 4th Baron Fermoy. The wedding took place in Westminster Abbey two years after the Coronation and was a regal affair, attended by 1,500 guests, including the Queen, Prince Philip, the Queen Mother and Princess Margaret. The bride was eighteen; the

Earl and Countess Spencer at Althorp on 15 September 1978

King William's Room, Althorp

Above: Viscount Althorp and his fiancée The Hon. Frances Roche, 28 May 1954

Right: Maurice Fermoy, the 4th Baron, in 1930

groom was twelve years older. She was the youngest girl to have been married in the Abbey for fifty years.

The bride's parents had been tenants of King George V and King George VI, living on the Sandringham estate in Park House, and it was here that Viscount Althorp's children were born and brought up. Their first child was Elizabeth Sarah Lavinia (Lady Sarah) born in 1955. Then came Cynthia Jane (Lady Jane), born in 1957. A wished-for son and heir died at birth in January 1960, and so the arrival of a *third* daughter on Saturday, 1 July 1961, was a temporary disappointment. She was christened Diana Frances at Sandringham, with Lady Mary Coleman, one of the Queen's nieces, and formerly Lady Mary Bowes-Lyon, as her godmother.

It was not the first time that the Royal Family had shown their esteem and affection for the Spencers in this way. The godparents of Lady Diana's sisters, Lady Sarah and Lady Jane, included, respectively, the Queen Mother and the Duke of Kent – the Queen herself is godmother to Lady Diana's young brother, Charles, born in 1964. Her father, the 8th Earl, was a godson of Queen Mary and the Duke of Windsor, and Edward VII was godfather to the 7th Earl. Other royal sponsors of Spencer children have been Queen Alexandra, Queen Maud of Norway, Queen Victoria (who was godmother of Victoria Alexandrina, daughter of the 4th Earl), George III and Queen Charlotte who were godparents to Georgiana Charlotte, daughter of the 2nd Earl, whose godfather in turn was George II.

To this day, the closeness of the royal connection is due in part to the long and valued friendship of two grandmothers – Lady Fermoy, maternal grandmother of Lady Diana, and the Queen Mother, maternal grandmother of Prince Charles – and to the friendship of Lord Fermoy and King George VI.

The Fermoys

Lady Diana's ancestors on her mother's side, the Fermoys, originated in Ireland, in County Cork, where Edmund Burke Roche was MP for Cork from 1837 to 1855. He was created Baron Fermoy in 1856. For a short period he then became MP for Marylebone in London and was ultimately Lord Lieutenant of County Cork. He married Miss Elizabeth Caroline Boothby, of Twyford Abbey near Acton, and was succeeded by his two sons: first of all by his eldest son, Edward FitzEdmund Burke, who became the 2nd Baron Fermoy, and then by his other son, James Boothby Burke.

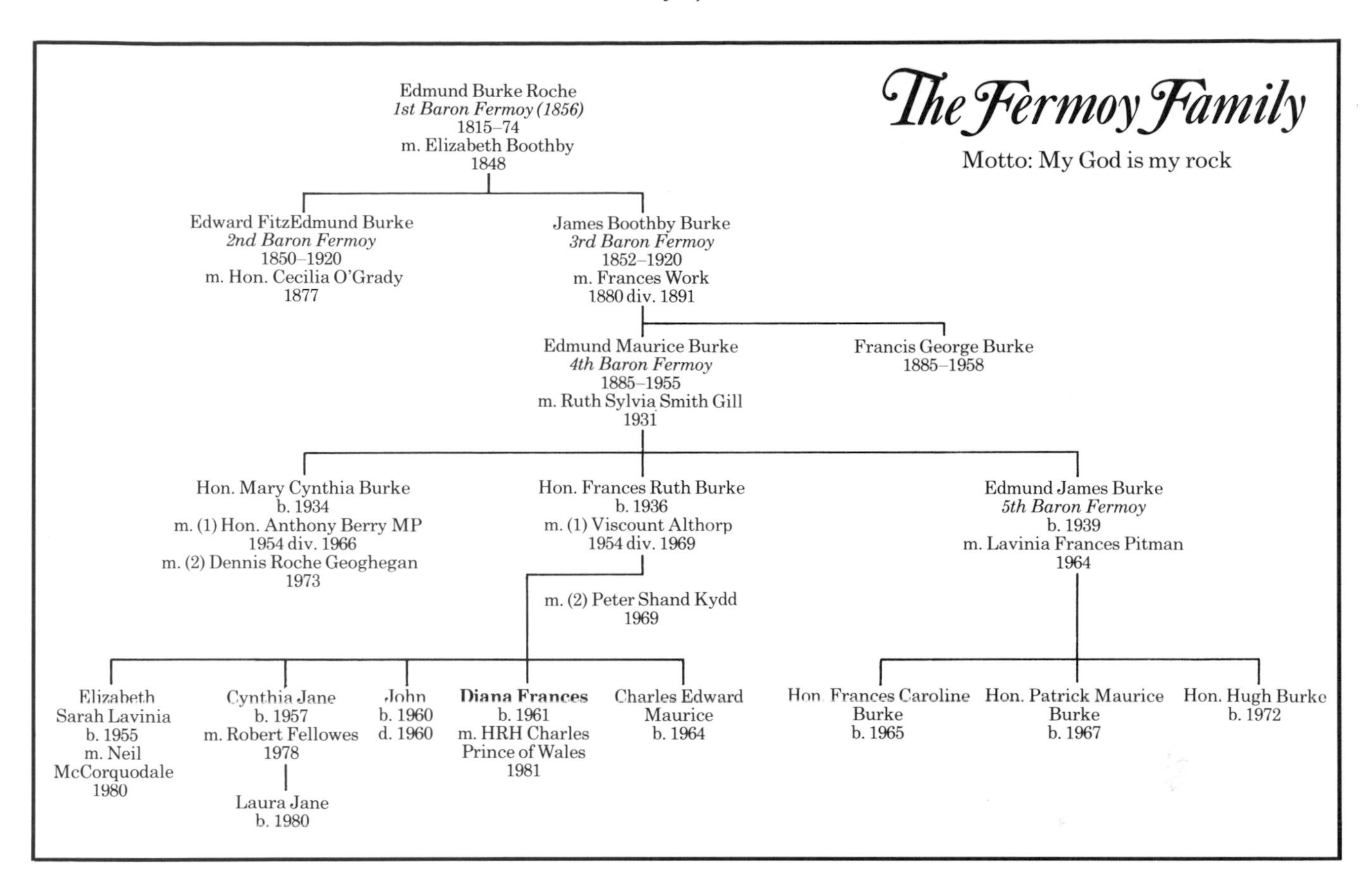

The 2nd Baron, Edward, who was born in 1850, married the Hon. Cecilia O'Grady, daughter of the 3rd Viscount Guillamore. They had no children, and when he died in September 1920, at the age of seventy, the title passed to his younger brother, James, then aged sixty-eight.

The 3rd Baron had married an American heiress, Frances Work, in 1880, the daughter of a wealthy New York businessman. She divorced James Fermoy in 1891, and their twin sons were brought up in America – a condition in their maternal grandfather's will. When Mr Work died, the boys were each left £600,000, provided they became American citizens within a year of his death and undertook never to visit England again. These conditions were later quashed by an American court, but the inheritance was reduced to £543,000, and the elder twin, Maurice, returned to his native country as the 4th Baron Fermoy. For in 1920, two months after the title had passed on his uncle's death to his father, who had become the 3rd Baron, James Fermoy died – and so his eldest son, aged thirty-five, succeeded to the baronetcy.

Maurice Fermoy, the 4th Baron and grandfather of Lady Diana, was born on 15 May 1885 in London – as was his identical twin, Francis, the younger by twenty minutes. They were educated at St Paul's School, Concord, New Hampshire, and at Harvard. Both were sportsmen and polo-players and belonged to various Harvard clubs, including the Kalumet, the AD Club and the Hasty Pudding Club. Maurice played ice-hockey; Francis rowed, being in the Sophomore and Newell Crews of 1905. Both graduated in 1909. For the 25th Anniversary Report on the Harvard Class of 1909, Maurice wrote: 'Immediately upon my graduation I took a trip through the National Parks of America, journeying on to Alaska. In the fall of 1909, I entered the offices of the Delaware, Lackawanna and Western RR, and remained there until I went to the Officers' Training Camp at Plattsburg, where I was commissioned a Captain and sent to Camp Dix, NJ. I went overseas with the 78th Division.' Francis, who served with the American Navy during World War I as a deck officer on Atlantic convoys, became a New York stockbroker and ultimately a banker in the Paris offices of the Guaranty Trust Company of New York; he never married. When their millionaire grandfather, Mr Work, died in 1911, the twins visited Europe and were in London in June 'to take in the Coronation of King George V'. Twenty-four years later Maurice Fermoy was the King's neighbour at Sandringham and a friend of his second son, who became King himself in 1936.

After Maurice returned to England as the 4th Baron Fermoy in 1921 and settled at Dersingham in Norfolk, he entered politics and became Conservative MP for King's Lynn in Norfolk, holding the

Lord Fermoy (on the right), with his twin and tennis partner, Francis, c. 1950 at Newport, Rhode Island

Lady Fermoy, as chairman of the King's Lynn Festival of Music and the Arts, with Yehudi Menuhin and the Mayor of King's Lynn

seat from 1924 to 1935 and for two years during World War II. At one time he was also Mayor of King's Lynn. On the outbreak of hostilities in 1939, he went to France with the YMCA and served meals to the troops, determined to play some useful part in the war. Later he joined the RAF, in which he served until he left to fight and win a by-election at King's Lynn in 1943.

In 1931, when he was forty-six, he married Ruth Sylvia Gill, daughter of William Smith Gill of Dalhebity, Bieldside in Aberdeenshire. They met in Paris, where she was studying the piano at the Conservatoire under Alfred Cortot. Her marriage robbed concert audiences of a fine musician and pianist. But when in 1951 she founded the King's Lynn Festival of Music and the Arts, she often took part in chamber music recitals with visiting artists in the Festival Ensemble – such as Sir John Barbirolli (who played the cello) and Raymond Leppard – and played duets with Gerald Moore. Lady Fermoy was Chairman of the Festival for twenty-five years. In 1963 she was made a Freeman of the Borough of King's Lynn.

The Fermoys had two daughters, Mary and Frances (Lady Diana's mother), and one son, Edmund James Burke, who was born in March 1939.

Apart from being an eager ice-hockey player, Maurice Fermoy, the 4th Baron, was a keen tennis-player, and became a friend of another tennis-player, the left-handed Duke of York, later George VI. The friendship developed when George V leased Park House, on the Sandringham estate, to Maurice Fermoy in 1935. It was in Park House that the Fermoy's younger daughter, Frances, was born, in January 1936 – on the same day that George V died. And it was in Park House, in 1961, that Frances, by then the wife of Viscount Althorp, gave birth to her youngest daughter, Diana – in the same bedroom where she herself had been born.

Maurice Fermoy's friendship with George VI lasted many years and was further cemented by the friendship of his wife, Ruth, with Queen Elizabeth. During World War II he used to play ice-hockey with the King against visiting American and Canadian troops on the Sandringham lakes, which were frozen over in winter. He was out hare shooting with the King on 5 February 1952, the day before the King died. After Baron Fermoy's death in 1955, his widow became an Extra Woman of the Bedchamber to Queen Elizabeth the Queen Mother in 1956, and four years later a Woman of the Bedchamber, a position she has held for over twenty years, to this day, becoming in the process a closer and more valued friend of the Queen Mother, herself grandmother of Prince Charles.

In 1954 the Hon. Frances Ruth Burke Roche married Viscount Althorp, later the 8th Earl Spencer. After her father's death and because of the long association and years of service of both the Fermoys and the Spencers, Park House was leased to Viscount Althorp and his wife in March 1955. Ruth Baroness Fermoy, having relinquished Park House, went to live in London. So it was that Lady Diana's mother returned to the house in which she had been born, thus continuing into the next generation the close association of the Windsors, the Spencers and the Fermoys; an association affirmed by the fact that the family at Park House were not just tenants but also friends and neighbours of the Royal Family whenever they came to stay at their own home in Norfolk.

The Queen Mother presenting Lady Diana's uncle, Edmund, the 5th Baron Fermoy, with the Grand Military Gold Cup at Sandown Park on 22 March 1961

Lady Diana's uncle, Edmund, who became the 5th Baron Fermoy at the age of sixteen while he was still at Eton, went to the Royal Military Academy at Sandhurst, becoming a captain in the Royal Horse Guards. He married Lavinia Frances Pitman, daughter of the late Captain John Pitman of Foxley House, near Malmesbury, in 1964, and settled at

Eddington House in Berkshire. They have three children: Frances, Maurice and Hugh, cousins of Lady Diana.

The Shand Kydds

Lady Diana's mother, the Hon. Frances Roche before she married Viscount Althorp in 1954, was born in 1936 and educated at Downham School, Hatfield Heath (now closed), where she was head-girl and captain of lacrosse, cricket, netball, and tennis. Like her father, the 4th Baron Fermoy, she was an excellent tennis-player, and in 1952 qualified in an inter-school knock-out competition for Junior Wimbledon. She was prevented from playing there, however, by an operation for appendicitis.

In 1969, her marriage to Viscount Althorp was dissolved, and she remarried later the same year at the age of thirty-three, her second husband being Peter Shand Kydd, then aged forty-four. It was also his second marriage, his first wife was a talented artist called Janet Munro Kerr, who painted many of the backdrops for a young, up-and-coming photographer, Antony Armstrong-Jones. Her grandfather was the eminent Edinburgh gynaecologist, John Martin Munro Kerr. Peter Shand Kydd's grandfather established a very successful business making quality wallpaper in the Shand Kydd factory in London where Polycell products were also invented and developed. The business was later merged and subsequently taken over, fifteen years ago, by Reed Decorative Products, a sub-division of Reed International.

Born in 1925, Peter Shand Kydd was educated at Marlborough College and Edinburgh University. He was fourteen at the start of World War II and joined the Royal Navy as soon as he could. He became a sub-lieutenant and served in four-man submarines, X-craft – despite his height of 6ft 3ins – in the seas around Scotland. He also served in the Pacific. At the war's end he acted as a liaison officer with the Italian Navy. In 1962 he left the family firm and emigrated to Australia with his first wife and their three children. They were there for three years, living on a sheep property near Young in New South Wales. Peter Shand Kydd also bought a property at Yass, 19 miles away, and sold the land at Young when he returned to England. After his second marriage in 1969 he and Frances Shand Kydd lived for two years in Sussex. In 1972 she bought a station next to his at Yass, and then in November they purchased a hill farm on the Isle of Seil, south of Oban, in Scotland, which is now their home. Mrs Shand Kydd has a toy shop, called Menzies, in Oban – which once misled a reporter into describing her as 'the manageress of a well-known stationers' – and helps her husband run their farms in Australia and Scotland.

The Hon. Mrs Peter Shand Kydd, Lady Diana's mother

CHAPTER 4

The Bridegroom

Prince Charles is one of the richest young men in England but he carries no money on his person. If necessary, there are equerries and secretaries in attendance to put their hands in their pockets on his behalf. Yet that seldom happens, for the Prince's daily routine is so pre-planned (up to a year in advance) that unforeseen eventualities are rare.

As he grasps the twin nettles of tradition and the twentieth century, no one is more aware of his uncomfortable position than the Prince himself. Despite his busy days and packed schedules he is without a substantial role. 'I don't really know what my role in life is,' he once said. 'At the moment, I don't have one. But somehow I must find one for myself.' As a consequence, he constantly appears to be earnestly attempting to establish his credentials, his worthiness and general preparedness for his only true mission in life: to be king. Until then he must continue to reconcile the anomalies of his exalted position with the coarse facts of the post-war world.

His Royal Highness, Prince Charles, the Prince of Wales, is also the Earl of Chester, Duke of Cornwall, Duke of Rothesay, Earl of Carrick, Baron of Renfrew, Lord of the Isles, Great Steward of Scotland, and heir to the throne.

He is Knight of the Most Noble Order of the Garter, Knight of the Most Ancient and Most Noble Order of the Thistle, Great Master and Principal Knight Grand Cross of the Most Honourable Order of the Bath, Commander Royal Navy, Wing Commander Royal Air Force, Colonel-in-Chief to ten regiments and Personal Aide-de-Camp to Queen Elizabeth II.

His chief source of income comes from the Duchy of Cornwall, which he inherited when his grandfather King George VI died in 1952. The Duchy of Cornwall and the title were instituted by Edward III in 1337 to provide a steady income for his eldest son, Edward of Woodstock, the Black Prince. In all, the Duchy now owns and manages nearly 129,000 acres in the West Country, possessions of feudal proportions: in Cornwall, 26,000 acres; on the Isles of Scilly, 4,100; in Devon, 72,085 acres. There are 16,460 acres in Somerset; 3,840 in Dorset; 3,960 in Wiltshire, and 1,240 acres in Gloucestershire. The Duchy is also proprietor of 45 acres of Kennington in London, including the Oval cricket-ground.

Prince Charles, Commander in the Royal Navy. He became Commander in January 1977.

Everything the Prince does is scrutinized by monarchists as much as by republicans, both closely watching his progress along the royal tightrope, wearing the awkward hat of Prince of Wales. Several former Princes have slipped and fallen; most recently his great-uncle, David, latterly the Duke of Windsor. There was also Queen Victoria's eldest son 'Bertie', later Edward VII, who waited in the wings for sixty years, with nothing very much to do but to spend money, and sought some escape and freedom in frivolous distractions.

The Victorian historian, Walter Bagehot, observed: 'All the world and the glory of it, whatever is most attractive, whatever is most seductive, has always been offered to the Prince of Wales of the day, and always will be. It is not rational to expect the best virtue, where temptation is applied in the most trying form at the frailest time of human life.'

It is almost as if Prince Charles has spent his youth and young adulthood trying to disprove this dictum. At the same time, he has striven to overcome the spectres of anachronism and dilettantism that have haunted his predecessors by notching up an impressive list of royal 'firsts'.

He is the first Prince of Wales to have gone to a school, to have gained a university degree, to have led a national sports team, to have trained as a commando and frogman, made a parachute jump and captained his own ship. Not only is he the first to have flown helicopters and supersonic jets, he has logged nearly 1,000 flying hours in an extraordinary array of aircraft: Vulcans, Phantoms, Hunters, Andovers, Buccaneers, Chipmunks and Harrier T4s.

He has also contributed to numerous books (mainly forewords), including scholarly historical works, wildlife manuals, humorous anthologies, and has even indulged in a little journalism. In addition, he is an active contributor to and campaigner for countless worthy causes, being president, patron or simply a member of approximately 200 charities, clubs and innumerable committees.

Despite all this, and his patent image of being a conscientious, dutiful person, rather than a charismatic playboy, the public's view of him is coloured by as much wish-fulfilling fantasy as that bestowed on any film-star. But he, more than most men, cannot be what he is or would really like to be; he must remain an institution rather than an individual, an institution invested with all the wealth and woes of his predecessors, along with the glamour, scandal, gossip, prejudices, misconceptions and legend.

This is why this Prince of Wales, one of the world's most privileged beings, takes a solitary, frugal breakfast every morning after a run and cold shower, and when at home in Buckingham Palace used to dine alone in his apartments, more often than not with a plate of scrambled eggs on his knees while watching television.

Prince Charles was born on Sunday evening, 14 November 1948, in Buckingham Palace. His energetic father, Prince Philip, played a game of squash while waiting for his first child to be born.

From the start there was a break with tradition, for King George VI had decreed that the custom of having a Minister of State present to witness the birth of an heir to the throne should in the case of his eldest daughter's child be abandoned. This custom dated back to 1688 and the 'warming-pan baby' controversy concerning James II's Roman Catholic wife, Mary of Modena, who was alleged to have introduced a changeling as heir in a warming-pan. George VI decided that a ministerial presence was 'merely the survival of an archaic custom'.

On the night of Prince Charles's birth, large crowds gathered outside the Palace, celebrating noisily till the early hours, and requests for them to quieten down, so that mother and baby (who weighed 7lb 6oz) could get some rest, did nothing to dampen their enthusiasm for the arrival of a prince in post-war Britain. The fountains in Trafalgar Square spouted blue for a boy; bonfires blazed; battleships of the British fleet fired 21-gun salutes, and as telegrams and messages carried the news around the globe, all over the still extant Empire bells pealed, as did those of St Paul's and Westminster Abbey in London. In the House of Commons, the Prime Minister, Mr Attlee, rose to hail the event, and he was followed by Winston Churchill, who employed his most ringing tones to greet 'the little Prince, now born into this world of strife and storm'.

Prince Charles was christened one month later, and because the Palace chapel, destroyed by a German bomb, had not yet been repaired, the ceremony was held in the Music Room, where a font which had been made for the baptism of Queen Victoria's first child in 1840 was set up after being brought from Windsor. It was Princess Margaret who placed the infant in the arms of the Archbishop of Canterbury and announced that his names were to be 'Charles Philip Arthur George'.

Under the direction of two Scottish nannies, Prince Charles had a healthy, normal, untroubled infancy. His parents soon moved out of Buckingham Palace into the newly refurbished Clarence House overlooking The Mall, and from there he was taken in a pram by a nanny and wheeled about St James's Park. Princess Anne was born on 15 August 1950, when Charles was one year and nine months old, and

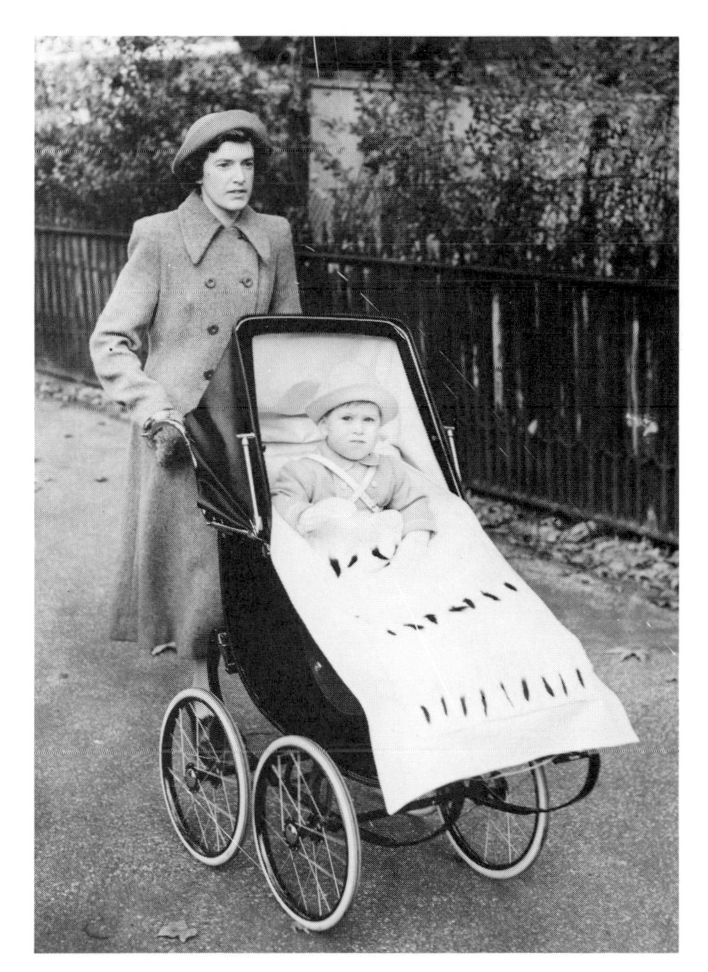

Left: Prince Charles was christened on 15 December 1948. He is held by his mother, Princess Elizabeth, while his grandfather, George VI, and great-grandmother, Queen Mary, look on.

Right: Prince Charles with his nannie, Miss Mabel Anderson, in Green Park on his second birthday

Left: Prince Charles showing musical talent at an early age

Right: Prince Charles witnessed part of the coronation of his mother in Westminster Abbey in June 1952.

the Prince was credited by his proud parents with taking 'a most watchful, protective interest' in his sister from the start.

The routine of the royal nursery was strict and unchanging. Up at 7 a.m.; breakfast; play till 9 a.m.; half an hour with mother; a walk in the park; lunch; then more fresh air until 4.30 p.m., when Princess Elizabeth would spend an hour-and-a-half with her children, helping to bath them before reading them bedtime stories. Although time with his mother was limited from the start, the Prince's ties with her have always been close. Indeed, despite a lack of domesticity (or because of it), he has always been much attached to his home and his family, a fact proved later in life by his reluctance to set up a separate bachelor base and by living instead with his parents. 'I've never wanted *not* to have a home life – to get away from home,' he has said. 'I *love* my home life. We happen to be a very close-knit family. I'm happier at home, with the family, than anywhere else.'

On 6 February 1952, King George VI died peacefully in his sleep at Sandringham. The new Queen returned hurriedly from a Commonwealth tour and in June, at her coronation, Prince Charles, now heir to the throne, was allowed into Westminster Abbey by a side-entrance to witness part of the ceremony. Afterwards, he appeared on the balcony of Buckingham Palace alongside his mother to acknowledge the cheering crowds.

As he himself has described it, the realization of his unique position was a gradual, but relentless process: 'I didn't wake up in my pram one day and say "Yippee!" It's something that dawns on you with the most ghastly, inexorable sense . . . and slowly you get the idea that you have a certain duty and responsibility . . .'

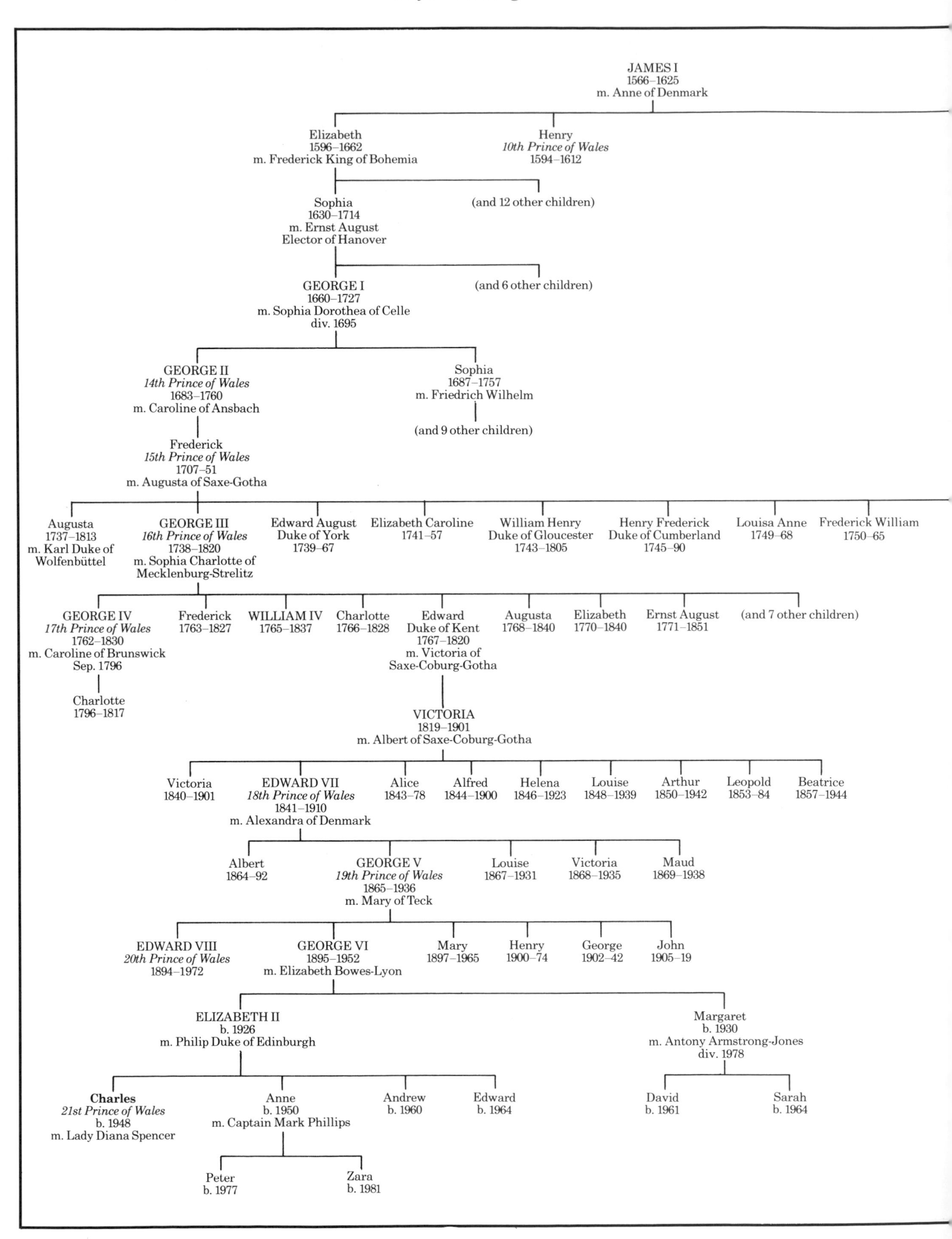
JAMES I
1566–1625
m. Anne of Denmark
Elizabeth
1596–1662
m. Frederick King of Bohemia
Henry
10th Prince of Wales
1594–1612
Sophia
1630–1714
m. Ernst August
Elector of Hanover
(and 12 other children)
GEORGE I
1660–1727
m. Sophia Dorothea of Celle
div. 1695
(and 6 other children)
GEORGE II
14th Prince of Wales
1683–1760
m. Caroline of Ansbach
Sophia
1687–1757
m. Friedrich Wilhelm
(and 9 other children)
Frederick
15th Prince of Wales
1707–51
m. Augusta of Saxe-Gotha
Augusta
1737–1813
m. Karl Duke of
Wolfenbüttel
GEORGE III
16th Prince of Wales
1738–1820
m. Sophia Charlotte of
Mecklenburg-Strelitz
Edward August
Duke of York
1739–67
Elizabeth Caroline
1741–57
William Henry
Duke of Gloucester
1743–1805
Henry Frederick
Duke of Cumberland
1745–90
Louisa Anne
1749–68
Frederick William
1750–65
GEORGE IV
17th Prince of Wales
1762–1830
m. Caroline of Brunswick
Sep. 1796
Frederick
1763–1827
WILLIAM IV
1765–1837
Charlotte
1766–1828
Edward
Duke of Kent
1767–1820
m. Victoria of
Saxe-Coburg-Gotha
Augusta
1768–1840
Elizabeth
1770–1840
Ernst August
1771–1851
(and 7 other children)
Charlotte
1796–1817
VICTORIA
1819–1901
m. Albert of Saxe-Coburg-Gotha
Victoria
1840–1901
EDWARD VII
18th Prince of Wales
1841–1910
m. Alexandra of Denmark
Alice
1843–78
Alfred
1844–1900
Helena
1846–1923
Louise
1848–1939
Arthur
1850–1942
Leopold
1853–84
Beatrice
1857–1944
Albert
1864–92
GEORGE V
19th Prince of Wales
1865–1936
m. Mary of Teck
Louise
1867–1931
Victoria
1868–1935
Maud
1869–1938
EDWARD VIII
20th Prince of Wales
1894–1972
GEORGE VI
1895–1952
m. Elizabeth Bowes-Lyon
Mary
1897–1965
Henry
1900–74
George
1902–42
John
1905–19
ELIZABETH II
b. 1926
m. Philip Duke of Edinburgh
Margaret
b. 1930
m. Antony Armstrong-Jones
div. 1978
Charles
21st Prince of Wales
b. 1948
m. Lady Diana Spencer
Anne
b. 1950
m. Captain Mark Phillips
Andrew
b. 1960
Edward
b. 1964
David
b. 1961
Sarah
b. 1964
Peter
b. 1977
Zara
b. 1981

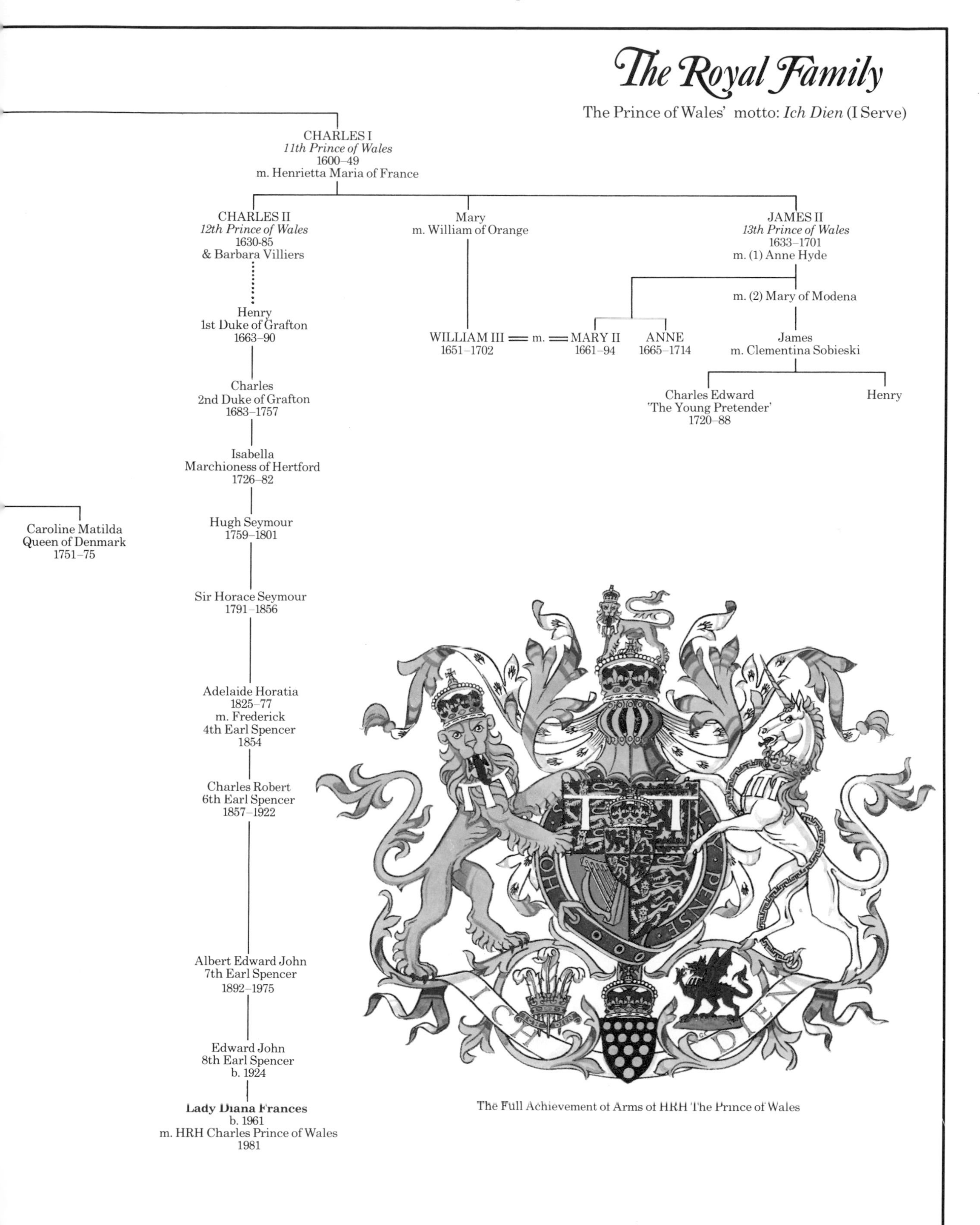

The Full Achievement of Arms of HRH The Prince of Wales

But already his upbringing was proceeding along much less formal paths than that of previous princelings. The Queen did not require her children to bow or curtsey to her, as tradition required, and as she had had to do before her own father when he became King. The Palace staff were instructed to address her son as 'Charles'. When he misbehaved he was spanked by nanny as well as by father – once by the latter for sticking his tongue out at crowds lining The Mall.

This pleasant, sheltered nursery life, where a fondness for painting and dressing-up soon evinced itself, came to an end when he was eight. To enlarge his horizons and make him a prince of his time – his cocooned existence meant that he had never been in a shop or on a bus – the Queen and Prince Philip resolved to make another radical break with royal tradition and to send Prince Charles to school with boys of his own age.

The boys at Hill House in Hans Place, Knightsbridge, were rather more than less of his own kind; a state education, after all, would have been much more destructive than instructive. Nevertheless, when Prince Charles was driven to school on 28 January 1957, it caused a sensation in the press.

For three days the school was virtually under siege, and the Queen feared she might have to abandon what she had thought of as an experiment. But after consultations with Fleet Street editors, the squads of pressmen were withdrawn and the new boy, registered as No. 102, was able to mingle with his class-mates. The aims of the school, outlined in a notice by the front door, were typically sensible ones for those boys being groomed to become members of the ruling class, if not to reign: 'A sense of rivalry has to be encouraged and a boy must be led to discover something in which he can excel. He must be trained to act quickly in an emergency, have the strength and ability to extract himself from a dangerous situation – and the urge to win.'

The Prince learned to play cricket and football, although swimming was his favourite sport. His favourite subjects were art and history. But in the classroom, as on the sports field, he did not excel. His parents, however, were well pleased: the object of the exercise was not to turn him into a scholar but to teach him how to mix with and relate to people outside the very restricted environment of the Court.

At the end of the first term his parents attended the school Field Day, and Prince Charles still remembers the thrill of hearing his father's shout of 'Well done, Charles!' as he competed in a team event.

Above: Painting of Prince Charles by Ludmilla Trapp, 1952

Below: Prince Charles and Princess Anne arrive at Ballater Station after a holiday at Balmoral in 1953.

His first school report, for Lent 1957, provides a guide to his progress and achievements:

Reading: Very good indeed. Good expression.
Writing: Good. Firm, clear, well-formed.
Arithmetic: Below form average. Careful but slow, not very keen.
Scripture: Shows keen interest.
Geography: Good.
History: Loves this subject.
French: Shows promise.
Latin: Made a fair start.
Art: Good, and simply loves drawing and painting.
Singing: A sweet voice, especially in the lower register.
Football: Enjoying the game.
Gymnastics: Good.

Prince Philip did not pay much attention to school reports. As he once explained: 'I say: "Look, I'm only going to bother if you're bottom. I really couldn't care less where you are. Just stay in the middle. That's all I ask."'

Arithmetic always continued to be Charles's major academic problem. Nearly twenty years later, in 1976, after being awarded an honorary Doctorate of Letters, he reminisced: 'I remember with terrifying clarity failing "O" Level Maths three times until, with superhuman effort, I passed on the fourth attempt . . . No one, least of all myself, likes to fail. But there is a great sense of achievement when success eventually comes.'

What would follow Hill House? Would his parents, having sent their son to a day-school like other boys, go further and send him to live as a boarder among boys of his own age and older? Top peoples' sons tend to follow in their father's footsteps in their schooling unless the mother objects or financial circumstances have changed. It was nonetheless another bold decision by his parents to send Prince Charles as a boarder to the Duke of Edinburgh's old preparatory school, Cheam, in Hampshire.

One of the obvious and powerful influences on Prince Charles's life has been his father, whom he not only greatly admires, to the extent of imitating his mannerisms, even his voice, but also regards with something like awe. Thus, while striving to emulate his rather daunting example, his eldest son also tries to prove himself by competing against that standard and trying to surpass it. Nonetheless, Prince Charles was never, as he says, 'made to follow in my father's footsteps . . . His attitude was very simple: he told me

The Prince returns to Hill House School after the Easter holidays in May 1957.

The Queen and Prince Charles at Badminton Horse Trials in April 1961

what were the pros and cons of all the possibilities and attractions and told me what he thought best. Then he left me to decide. I freely subjected myself to what he thought best because I saw how wise he was.'

However, the young Prince must have had many misgivings about his father's wisdom during his first days at England's oldest preparatory school: they were the unhappiest of his life. Pupil No. 89 – 'very much in need of a haircut' – was delivered by his parents to Cheam on 23 September 1957 and thrust unceremoniously into the spartan reality of the English private school system: uncarpeted dormitories with springless beds, hard, horse-hair mattresses, and little room for tender feelings and sensitive souls. Reveille was at 7.15 a.m.; prayers at 7.45 a.m.; and breakfast at 8 a.m.

The Prince later defended this kind of education with the polite commonsense that characterizes many of his public pronouncements. 'I suppose I could have gone to the local comprehensive or the local grammar, but I'm not sure it would have done me much good. I think a public school gives you a great deal of self-discipline and experience and responsibility, and it is the responsibility which is so worthwhile. It's very rewarding and it gives you the added confidence in yourself that you have the ability to do something for other people, and they trust you to do it. I think this is very important.'

Not surprisingly, with ancestors going back to Charlemagne, the young Prince's aptitude for history was by now fully confirmed. 'I've always been interested in history, even when I was quite small,' he confessed. 'I do not know whether it's me, or being born into what I was, but I *feel* history. It fascinates me. I'm a romantic at heart really.'

Being interested in history was one thing; being a part of it was another, as he learned in the summer of 1958 at the end of his first year at Cheam.

The Queen was to have performed the closing ceremony of the Commonwealth Games in Cardiff, but was prevented from doing so by a sinus operation. The Duke of Edinburgh took her place. Prince Charles and some other boys were allowed into the headmaster's study to watch the ceremony on television. At the Games Prince Philip introduced a taped message from Her Majesty – which was as much of a surprise to the small group at Cheam as it was to the crowd of 36,000 in the Cardiff stadium. For the Queen was heard to say: 'I intend to create my son Charles, Prince of Wales today.' In Cardiff the stadium erupted in applause and song as the Welsh crowd broke into 'God Bless the Prince of Wales'. At Cheam among the small group of boys, the new Prince of Wales went red in the face and wished he was anything else but that.

'I remember being acutely embarrassed when it was announced,' he later recalled. 'I heard this marvellous great cheer coming from the stadium in Cardiff, and I think for a little boy of nine it was rather bewildering. All the others turned and looked at me in amazement. Perhaps it didn't mean all that much then. Later on, as I grew older, it became apparent what it meant.'

He had just got used to Cheam when on 1 May 1962 he was sent even further away from home to the harsher environment of Gordonstoun. His father took him there, flying his own plane to Lossiemouth and then driving his thirteen-year-old son to the school.

Although the decision to send the Prince of Wales there to complete his education was taken by 'all the family', it was Prince Philip who prevailed. Once again, it was his old public school, one where he had shone and been happy. But the difference in character between father and son meant that where the extrovert sportsman had thrived, the more studious, artistic and self-conscious boy was not at all at home. He later told friends he was 'rather unhappy' for the first few years, and then 'rather bored'. At first, he said, he found the school 'pretty gruesome'.

The regime at Gordonstoun was bleak; the school's motto was: 'There is more in you'. The dormitories were unpainted, the floorboards bare, the light bulbs

Prince Charles arrives at Gordonstoun, his new school, in Scotland, accompanied by Prince Philip in 1962. They are greeted by the headmaster, Mr Robert Chew.

without shades and the bedsteads of wood. The day began at 7 a.m. with a run round the garden, whatever the weather, followed by an ice-cold shower. Breakfast was at 8.15, prayers at 8.55. Morning classwork was followed at 1.20 by lunch and a twenty-minute rest period. In the afternoon there were sports, seamanship, or estate work three days a week, and one day a week was devoted to some public service, such as scouting, the fire service, mountain rescue, coastguard-watching, army cadets or surf life-saving. Supper was at 6.20 p.m. and lights out at 9.30 p.m.

In vain the young Prince asked the Queen Mother to intercede with his parents on his behalf and persuade them to remove him. He stayed where he was and began to adapt and learn.

'I'm glad I went to Gordonstoun,' said Prince Charles later. 'It wasn't the toughness of the place – that's all much exaggerated by reports – it was the general character of the education there . . . which tries to balance the physical and mental, with an emphasis on self-reliance to develop a rounded human being. Gordonstoun developed my will-power and self-control. It helped me to discipline myself, and I think that discipline, not in the sense of making you bath in cold water, but in the Latin sense – giving shape and form and tidiness to your life – is the most important thing your education can do . . . I believe it taught me a great deal about myself and my own abilities and disabilities, and it taught me to take challenges and initiatives.'

In his first term the Prince ended 'very near the top of his form'. The plodder was showing grit and determination. Despite his dislike of group activities and team games, Prince Charles perforce 'mucked in' and joined in all the tough and rugged outdoor activities. He developed new interests, including pottery-making and playing the trumpet and the cello. In his spare time he learned to fish, shoot, and to play polo in the holidays.

After two years he managed to pass five 'O' Levels: English Language, English Literature, History, Latin and French. It was a very average achievement. All the same, it was another royal first. So was his debut as a player king, when in November 1965, a fortnight after his seventeenth birthday, he played the lead in the school's production of *Macbeth*. The audience enjoyed the spectacle of the Prince of Wales' bloody quest to be king, and so did the *Gordonstoun Record*, saying the Prince was at his best in the passages expressing Macbeth's terrible agony of remorse and fear – and added: 'He equally well expressed the degenerative hardening of Macbeth's character, the assumption of cynicism in an attempt to blunt the underlying and too painful moral sensitivity . . .'

The most notable if not notorious episode of Prince Charles's school career was what has come to be known as the 'Cherry Brandy Incident', which demonstrated how a tiny, banal event in the Prince's development could be inflated into a scandal of mock-heroic proportions. In June, 1963, while on a sailing expedition on the school yacht, *Pinta*, Prince Charles and four other boys landed at Stornoway, on the Isle of Lewis. They went to the Crown Hotel for lunch (accompanied, as always, by the Prince's bodyguard), and inevitably a crowd followed them. When Inspector Donald Green went off to arrange a visit to a cinema, Prince Charles tried to evade the stares of curious onlookers by escaping into an adjacent room, the bar. Unfortunately, the incident that followed was observed by a journalist and by the next morning the story had become a front page sensation.

'Well, I thought it was the end of the earth. I was all ready to pack my bags and leave for Siberia,' Prince Charles recalled. 'Having never been into a bar before, the first thing I thought of doing was having a drink of course. It seemed the most sensible thing. And being terrified, not knowing what to do, I said the first drink that came into my head, which happened to be a cherry brandy, because I'd drunk it before, when it was cold, out shooting. Hardly had I taken a sip when the whole world exploded around my ears. That's all.'

At the end of January 1966, he went to Australia. It was a turning-point. The Prince's first visit 'down-under' provided him with another kind of relief or liberation. 'Australia got me over my shyness,' was his simple summation of the welcome two-term break from Gordonstoun in 1966. He was now seventeen.

For some time the Royal Family had debated other means of extending the Prince's horizons. The previous year, the Australian Prime Minister, Sir Robert Menzies, had recommended a stay at Timbertop, the country offshoot of Geelong School near Melbourne, Australia's most exclusive Church of England grammar school. At Timbertop, 200 miles north of Melbourne and 2,000 feet above sea-level, 130 boys led a relaxed, adventurous, rural life, well away from the competitive pressures and chores of the classroom and in the Prince's case of a class-ridden society. They hiked across country and went for cross-country runs. There was plenty of fishing, as well as bird-watching, tree-felling, sheep-shearing, even gem-hunting and panning for gold.

Prince Charles loved it all. 'The most wonderful experience I've ever had,' he said. Originally he was to have stayed for just one term but so successful was this venture that the Prince at his own request was allowed to stay on for two. 'Australia opened my eyes,' he said. 'You are judged there on how people see you and feel about you. There are no assumptions there. Having a title and being a member of the upper classes as often as not mitigates against you. In Australia, you have to fend for yourself. I was fairly shy when I was younger but Australia cured me of that . . . That school's probably the reason why, whenever I come back to Australia, I experience a curious and inexplicable sense that I belong.'

A school trip to Papua in New Guinea was important for other reasons. When the plane landed at Port Moresby, a large crowd was waiting to greet the Prince, who panicked at the thought of having to face them on his own and in his own right. He virtually had to be kicked off the plane by his Palace aide, Squadron Leader David Checketts. But when he steeled himself to talk to them, he found he enjoyed it. Ever since, he says, he has had no fear of crowds.

After that, to return to Gordonstoun for a final year seemed something of an anti-climax. However, Prince Charles was now in a much better position to make the most of himself and his opportunities, and soon he was appointed 'guardian' or head-boy – a particular satisfaction as it was a position his father had held nearly thirty years before.

That summer the Prince took his 'A' Levels and gained creditable passes in French and History, with a distinction in the optional special paper. In so doing he proved he could win a university place for himself – yet another royal first.

Prince Charles spent two terms at Timbertop in Australia in 1966. He is seen here with Stuart McGregor, a sheep farmer's son and former headboy of Geelong, who shared a room with the Prince in the masters' quarters.

It was Prince Charles himself who made the final decision to go to university, and Trinity College, Cambridge, was the choice, partly because King George VI had been there fifty years before. The Master of the College was the distinguished former Conservative Home Secretary, Mr R.A.B. Butler, who had been created a life peer in 1965. He advised Prince Charles to follow his own interests and study anthropology and archaeology.

He went there in October 1967. By now he was much more at ease in public, and the crowds were beginning to respond to this young man who had lost his gauche appearance and that rather solemn, unsmiling public face. 'Good luck!' shouted someone from the crowd. The Prince waved back and grinned: 'I'll need it!'

While Prince Charles worked hard and steadily at his studies, he also pursued his old interests, such as music and acting, and made a few friends – although the Master of the College was disappointed to note that they still tended to be of the public school and polo-playing sort. He tried, however, to be a normal student, cycling to lectures and wearing baggy trousers and a leather-patched jacket.

He joined the college's dramatic group, the Dryden Society, and played the padre in Orton's comedy *Erpingham Camp*, and as such had a custard-pie flattened on his face. Later he took part in two revues.

In his second year at Cambridge he decided to switch subjects and study history. Lord Butler tried to dissuade him, pointing out that if he continued with archaeology or anthropology he might get a prized First. The Prince stuck to his guns, saying that he particularly wanted to study the British constitution. 'Why?' asked Butler. 'Because,' replied the Prince, 'I am probably going to be King.'

In July 1969 came the next big step towards this eventuality: his Investiture as the Prince of Wales at Caernarvon Castle. Partly in preparation for this, he went for one term to the University College of Wales in Aberystwyth, to study the history, language and problems of Wales and do a crash-course in Welsh. It was a decision that was met with a great deal of criticism in Wales itself, where many people felt that a firm hand was required instead to deal with the country's economic ills. There were demonstrations and bomb explosions. Prince Charles himself had misgivings about the venture. But in his dogged style, he knuckled down and studied so hard that by the end of the course he was able to address the Welsh League of Youth with a short, but allegedly faultless speech in Welsh.

Then on 1 July 1969, in a ceremony of impressive but cost-conscious pageantry, which was witnessed by some 500 million television viewers around the world, Prince Charles was formally invested as the Prince of Wales by his mother; and the announcement made eleven years before, which had so embarrassed the little boy at Cheam, was successfully realized. The climax of the ceremony came when the Prince knelt before his mother, placed his hands between hers, and payed homage thus: 'I, Charles, Prince of Wales, do become your liege man of life and limb and of earthly worship, and faith and truth I will bear unto you to live and die against all manner of folks.'

At university Prince Charles played an active part in his college's dramatic society.

After his Investiture, the twenty-first Prince of Wales returned to his studies at Trinity, and in June 1970 it was announced that 'Wales, HRH, Prince of' had gained a Bachelor of Arts degree in history – Class 2, Division 2. It was a more than creditable performance. The diligent student had come a long way by solid application to his tasks and sheer dint of effort and determination.

He now had to make use of and exploit his education. While other new graduates sought their first jobs, his prospects were no less uncertain. He

Overleaf: Prince Charles was invested as Prince of Wales at Caernarvon Castle on 1 July 1969.

RED DRAGON II
OPEN

Above: Prince Charles gives Prince Edward a ride on a go-kart at Windsor Castle. The Prince has always been very attached to his family.

Left: Prince Charles 'passes out' as a helicopter pilot at the Royal Naval Air Station at Yeovilton, Somerset, in December 1974. At this time he was a serving officer in the Royal Naval frigate HMS 'Jupiter'.

also had to find something to do. But for the rest of 1970 he went abroad on a series of royal tours and visits. Having already toured Japan in April, he travelled to Canada, America, France, Fiji, Bermuda, Barbados, Germany and Kenya before beginning to learn some skills as a modern warrior prince in the spring of 1971.

As Prince of Wales he had inherited the motto *Ich Dien* (I Serve), and this, he explained, was the basis of his job: 'to serve other people . . . If you have a sense of duty, and I like to think I have, service means that you give yourself to people, particularly if they want you – but sometimes if they don't.' In pursuit of this ideal it was decided he should follow royal tradition and enter the services – with a particular emphasis on the Royal Navy.

'I think the Navy meant a great deal to me because I was basically brought up in it,' said Prince Charles. 'My father was in it; my grandfather; my great-uncle, Lord Mountbatten; and my great-grandfathers, Prince Louis of Battenberg and King George V . . . Ultimately, our security and everything depends upon the Navy. It always has done throughout history and always will.'

But first he went to the RAF College, Cranwell, in March 1971, to do some advanced jet-training. He was given the rank of flight lieutenant and his course was given the grandiose code-name 'Operation Golden Eagle'. He had already done some flying at Cambridge, having clocked up 180 flying hours, and in August, after parachuting (this was optional) into Studland Bay off Dorset, he was proficient enough to be presented with his 'wings'.

In October he moved on to the Royal Naval College, Dartmouth, to do a six-week graduate course with the rank of acting sub-lieutenant. He passed out top in navigation and seamanship, and joined the guided-missile destroyer *Norfolk* in Gibraltar in November 1971 as a sub-lieutenant. Over the next four years he served on a number of ships, including a coastal mine-sweeper, HMS *Glasserton*, the frigates *Minerva* and *Jupiter* and the commando aircraft-carrier HMS *Hermes*.

His time with the Fleet Air Arm was the most enjoyable of his career, and it is in this branch of the services that he would most like to have worked. He said later: 'I adore flying – and I personally cannot think of a better combination than Navy flying – being at sea and being able to fly at the same time. I found it very exciting, very rewarding and very stimulating. Also bloody terrifying sometimes . . . People who fly in the Fleet Air Arm are a very special breed. [They] are some of the most invigorating and amusing people I've met.'

In February 1976, the Prince of Wales, aged twenty-seven, was given his own command, and took his place on the bridge as captain of the mine-hunter, HMS *Bronington*, one of the Navy's smallest ships, with a crew of four officers and thirty-three men. For ten months he and his command patrolled the North Sea on the look-out for wartime mines. He said later that those months had given him 'a marvellous opportunity to get as close to the "ordinary" British chap as possible.'

Indeed, those under his command responded warmly to him, recognizing his qualities of leadership, his technical skills and humanity. His outward appearance also reflected the sea-change: he was lean and superbly fit, with an altogether tougher and more businesslike look about him. His manner was crisp and positive. In his naval uniform, the Prince of Wales looked every inch the classic image of a young British naval hero. One of his proudest moments was when his father, the Admiral of the Fleet, paid his ship a visit in Rosyth.

When Prince Charles retired from active service in December 1976, after five years in the Navy, he was given an affectionate, rumbustious send-off, and his crew launched their captain back into civvy street with a lavatory seat, in lieu of a throne, around his neck.

In January 1977 he was promoted to commander in the Royal Navy and became a wing commander in the RAF. But his duties were now directed towards public service and along the path of royal visits, appearances and tours.

In April 1977 he launched the Queen's Silver Jubilee Appeal as its president and helped to raise £16 million. He was installed as Chancellor of the University of Wales that July, and in December was appointed to Her Majesty's Privy Council. But his exact function, use and role remain uncertain and he has still not found a completely sustaining, creative and substantial job.

He has to behave and generally fulfil his role as heir to the throne. He has to obey the dictates of tradition, while trying to reconcile the new, and often conflicting, demands and hopes of the public, the Palace and Parliament. At the same time, the Prince must remain true to himself. 'I was asked in Australia whether I concentrated on improving my image – as if I was some kind of washing-powder,' he said. He once tried to explain his rather rarified life-style with these words: 'Some of the sailors used to say: "Wouldn't you like a life of your own? Wouldn't

Left: Prince Charles in command of the mine-hunter HMS 'Bronington' in March 1976

Right: The Queen's Silver Jubilee Thanksgiving Service on 7 June 1977. Prince Charles was President of the Queen's Silver Jubilee Appeal.

Overleaf: Prince Charles is an expert polo-player: he is seen here playing at Jaipur in India.

4

Prince Charles is skilled at many sports besides polo: he is seen above shooting on the National Rifle Association's ranges at Bisley in Surrey.

you like to be able to go down to the pub?" My favourite occupation is *not* going down to the pub . . . I have got a life of my own and I like it. Perhaps I would like another life more, but this is the one I know.'

What the Prince likes to do when he is off-duty is to indulge in the traditional leisure activities of the aristocracy – hunting, fishing and shooting, and playing polo. At all these sports he is first-rate. Although Prince Charles dislikes his nick-name 'Action Man', it is one that his abilities invite. Recently he has been criticized for taking greater and greater risks, particularly with his new passion for steeplechasing. He admits: 'Perhaps I push myself too much. But it is my outlook on life.' The reason, he also realizes, could be 'because I am constantly feeling that I have to justify myself, my existence. I want to prove to myself that I can accept challenges, and that I can mentally accept things which are perhaps dangerous or slightly frightening.' Prince Charles is acutely aware of the difficult path he has to pick between the dictates of the past and the demands of the present and future. That he has to work hard to keep a proper balance and yet succeeds so well is perhaps the best guarantee for the future.

Now, as he embarks upon a new venture, and establishes a family life of his own, doubtless his role will become clearer, and more light will be shed on what we may expect when one day he ascends the throne. His Royal Highness, Prince Charles, the Prince of Wales, says simply: 'This particular job is what I make it – you'll have to see what I do with it.'

Left: Prince Charles at a polo match at Smith's Lawn, Windsor

CHAPTER 5

The Friends of the Bride and Groom

If the books that someone reads can tell you something about that reader's interests and character, so can a person's friends. One way of learning something about the life-styles, preferences and personalities of Prince Charles and Lady Diana is to look at the people they have as friends – people who come from a very exclusive but enduring club, the landed aristocracy of Britain.

Despite creeping socialism and the erosion of position and wealth, this world of country-house society, of lords and ladies, of weekend parties and polo and public schools, of the Guards and the City, of horses and hunting, of good manners, good friends and good fun – this world, one per cent of the population, still thrives. It carries on regardless, not inviting inspection and trying to avoid the attention of others.

The Queen is a part of this special yet not especially gifted society, a country-house owner of unimaginable wealth, and one of the richest women in the world. Yet at heart she is still a country-woman who loves country pursuits and people and places. Her eldest son's background is the same and his likings are similar, although spiced with a male aristocrat's ardour for risking his neck. His wife was also born and brought up in this hard-working and cheerfully hedonistic world – as were their friends.

Lady Diana

By her own admission, the three best friends of Lady Diana Spencer are the three girls who shared her London flat in Coleherne Court in South Kensington. Carolyn Pride, Anne Bolton and Virginia Pitman were and are a loyal and trusted trio, and Lady Diana relied greatly on their moral support and discretion during the months before the engagement. They all have very different interests, but their backgrounds, attitudes and aspirations, as with all Lady Diana's other friends, are much the same.

Lady Diana's three best friends, Virginia Pitman, Carolyn Pride, and Anne Bolton who shared her flat in Coleherne Court

Carolyn Pride is an exact contemporary of Lady Diana – they were at West Heath at the same time. At school, she was a competitive horse-rider, winning several junior hunter trials. She is now in the middle of a four-year graduate course at the Royal College of Music, where she is specializing in singing. She is also an accomplished pianist. A Friend of Covent Garden, she is keen on ballet. In the summer she plays tennis and in the winter, when time and funds permit, she skis.

Anne Bolton is a year older than Lady Diana. After taking 'O' Levels at St Mary's School in Wantage, Oxfordshire, she went to the Oxford and County Secretarial College. She liked the Oxford life and stayed there an extra year, working for a property company, before moving to London. She now works for the estate agents, Savills. After Lady Diana's engagement, she told a BBC television reporter, who asked her if it had been difficult to keep quiet: 'It was very easy. Terribly easy. The most difficult thing was knowing that it was actually going to take place. We wanted everyone to be as happy as we were. So we wanted to tell everyone – but obviously we couldn't.' Asked what Lady Diana had said, Anne Bolton replied: 'She literally said: "I'm engaged." And from that moment on she didn't get a chance to say much.'

Aged twenty-one, Virginia Pitman is probably the most adventurous of the four flatmates. Educated at Hatherop Castle, a school in Gloucestershire, noted more for its setting than its academic record, she went on to take a Cordon Bleu cooking-course. She then cooked directors' lunches, before training as a restorer of antique china. She is now qualified and works in South Kensington not far from the flat. Virginia is a keen amateur photographer and has a fine collection of photographs recording a hitch-hiking trip she made from her home in Wensleydale, Yorkshire, through Europe to North Africa. 'We shall miss her most dreadfully,' said Virginia after

Lady Diana had left Coleherne Court. 'We knew for some time that she was going out with Prince Charles. She never tried to cover up who she was seeing . . . Of course we talked about the romance between ourselves. And when she was upset by all the pressures on her, we would talk about it and try to decide the best thing to do.'

As Lady Diana only left school four years ago, most of her girl-friends tend to be school-friends or girls who have shared her upbringing in some way. She has known Alexandra Loyd all her life, as Alexandra was brought up at Sandringham, where her father, Julian, is the Queen's land agent. The two girls went initially to Sylfield School in King's Lynn as day-girls, then on to Riddlesworth Hall as boarders. They often spent some part of their holidays together, sharing a common interest in country life. After Riddlesworth, their paths diverged when Alexandra went to St Mary's, Wantage. They continued to see each other during their holidays. Alexandra Loyd is a typical member of the Spencer Set: bright and positive, but no blue stocking, active without being sporty, and thoroughly competent in her work. She studied for her 'A' Levels at Queensgate in South Kensington and then went to the Marlborough Secretarial College, Cambridge. She now works for John Patten, Conservative MP for the city of Oxford.

Another close friend from school-days and Norfolk is the Hon. Caroline Harbord Hammond, the twenty-year-old daughter of Lord Suffield. Like many of Lady Diana's friends, the Harbord Hammonds have served the Royal Family. Caroline's father, a major in the Coldstream Guards, is a member of Her Majesty's Bodyguard of the Honourable Corps of Gentlemen at Arms, while her brother, Charles, a captain in his father's regiment, has been a temporary equerry to the Queen since 1977. Caroline was also a boarder at Riddlesworth Hall and went on with Lady Diana to West Heath, where among the school's activities they shared a competitive interest in swimming. She has spent several holidays on the Isle of Seil with Lady Diana, as the island is not far from her parents' cottage home on the Isle of Mull. She now has a permanent job in the press department of the Conservative Central Office.

Other firm and lifelong friends of Lady Diana are the Hon. Henry Malcolm Herbert and his sister Carolyn, the second son and younger daughter of Lord Porchester, the Queen's racing manager. Harry Herbert, now aged twenty-two, began acting at Eton, taking the lead in his House's productions of *London Assurance* and *The Jockey Club Stakes*. For his Leaver's play he played the headmaster in Alan Bennett's *Forty Years On*. After Eton he went to Paris to the Alliance Français to learn French. He narrowly missed being accepted by RADA but still acts with the Grenville Players in London. Their latest production, *The Reluctant Debutante*, by William Douglas Home, raised £4,500 for the Cancer Relief Fund. Like others in the Spencer Set he is socially aware and while still at Eton he supervised a discothèque for retarded children. He works for the stockbrokers, Rowe and Pitman.

His sister, Carolyn, is a few weeks younger than Lady Diana. From St Mary's, Wantage, she went on to St Clare's College, Oxford, where she studied for her 'A' Levels. In keeping with the traditional Herbert association with horses – her grandfather is the legendary amateur jockey and wit, the Earl of Caernarvon – she rides in three-day events. In between working for her father's stud farm she is studying for an 'A' Level in history of art. She enjoys travelling. The Herberts live near Newbury in Berkshire. The Queen attended a dance given for Harry and his sister at Highclere Castle, their grandfather's home, in 1980.

Sophie Kimball was Lady Diana's constant flatmate when they shared Mrs Shand Kydd's former London flat in Cadogan Place. Her father, Marcus Kimball, Conservative MP for Gainsborough and Chairman of the British Field Sports Society, is a former joint Master and Huntsman of the Fitzwilliam Hounds and a former joint Master of the Cottesmore – one of the best packs of foxhounds in the country, which includes the Prince of Wales as a member. The Kimballs' home is in Leicestershire and they have another house in the Scottish Highlands near Lairg, where Lady Diana has been a frequent visitor.

James Boughey (pronounced 'Bowey') is the younger brother of Sir John Boughey, who recently succeeded his father as the 11th Baronet. A dapper, fair-haired lieutenant in the Coldstream Guards, he was an early escort of Lady Diana, and like many of her men-friends, an Etonian. A 'dry-bob' – as cricketers are called at Eton – he distinguished himself by scoring a half century at Lords in the Eton/Harrow match in 1978. His family's motto 'Neither seek nor despise distinction' might well be applied to all Lady Diana's friends, some of whom, unabashed at the unusual distinction of being a friend of the *fiancée* of the Prince of Wales have, when questioned by the press, inadvertently and innocently allowed their candour to weaken that friendship.

Teresa Mowbray, god-daughter of Mrs Shand Kydd, was a year senior to Lady Diana at West Heath. After leaving school she assumed an appearance and style that distanced her from some of her contemporaries – a distance that widened temporarily when she chatted to the *Sunday Mirror* and the *News of the World*. She said: 'Diana was always telling me I looked a real sight – in a lighthearted

Harry Herbert is seen here with the Grenville Players. He is in the middle of the back row. Simon Berry is sitting on the left of the director.

way. She was always so immaculate, and her taste in clothes is impeccable . . . She's witty, charming, terribly domesticated and popular with everyone.'

Simon Berry, a charming and friendly Old Etonian, aged twenty-three, is the son of the chairman of the family wine business, Berry Brothers and Rudd, of St James's Street in London. He also spoke too openly of his three-year association with Lady Diana, and provided the *Sunday Mirror* with photographs of her on a skiing holiday with eighteen friends in the French Alps in 1979. His 'revelations' included the fact that Lady Diana did imitations of Miss Piggy, that she was popular with young men – 'Many have tried to win her, sending flowers and begging for a date; but she always politely declined.'

Prince Charles

The Prince of Wales' men-friends fall mainly into three categories: aristocrats with royal connections; academics of all ages and classes; and sportsmen associated with his favourite sports. Occasionally, a friendly acquaintance will move from the periphery into the inner sanctum of his friends after his loyalty has been proved. He himself has said: 'I tend to have a few, but very good friends . . . I trust my friends implicity, and they know that. The more discreet, the better.'

One such friend is Guy Wildenstein. He was a polo-playing acquaintance of the Prince of Wales, but has now graduated to that inner corps of his loyal friends. A year older than the Prince, immensely rich and slightly built, Wildenstein runs his father's well-known fine art galleries in London and Paris, as well as editing his own fine art magazine, *La Gazette des Beaux Arts*. This year Wildenstein bought 'The Holy Family' by Nicolas Poussin, offered for sale by the Duke of Devonshire at Christie's, for a record £1,650,000.

Since 1977, Prince Charles has played polo, as the No. 4 (the back or defensive man), for Wildenstein's not unsuccessful team *Les Diable Bleus* – the Blue Devils. Before that the Prince played for the Golden Eagles, the high-goal team of Louis Sosa Basualdo. Polo-players, who need to be very fit, well practised and skilled, are rated from −2 to 10, the latter being the highest rating. Prince Charles's current handicap is 4 and his father's is 5.

A good friend of Prince Charles is Lieutenant Colonel Andrew Parker-Bowles, of the Blues and Royals, with whom he has much in common. In the early 1970s 'the Captain' as Parker-Bowles was known then, was a close friend of Princess Anne. Impeccably well-mannered and well-bred, he is the son of the late Derek Parker-Bowles (a kinsman of the Earls of Macclesfield), and Dame Ann, former Chief Commissioner, Girl Guides, and a daughter of the race-horse owner, Sir Humphrey de Trafford. He was page to the Lord High Chancellor, Lord Simmonds, at the Coronation. After being educated at Ampleforth, he went to Sandhurst and was commissioned in the Blues in 1970. A good horseman, he played polo for his regiment and for the Army. In 1973 he married Camilla Shand, a former girlfriend of the Prince of Wales. In 1980, Andrew Parker-Bowles was promoted to Lieutenant Colonel and travelled to Rhodesia with Lord Soames, the country's last Governor General. He acted as the Liaison Officer with the Patriotic Front during the change-over of power that led to the country's independence.

The Parker-Bowles are among the closest friends of the Prince of Wales, providing what is known as 'a safe house' for him at their home, Bolehyde Manor, Allington, near Chippenham in Wiltshire.

Another member of the inner core of Prince Charles's friends is Hugh van Cutsem, the son of the

Guy Wildenstein shares an interest in polo with Prince Charles. He is seen here, on the extreme right, at Smith's Lawn, Windsor in 1980 with Prince Charles (centre).

2
2
2

Prince Charles was best man to Nicholas Soames at his wedding on 4 June 1981. The Prince is seen here with the Queen Mother, Princess Margaret and Lady Diana after the ceremony.

famous race-horse trainer, the late Bernard van Cutsem and Mary Compton. Hugh van Cutsem's wife, Emilie, is Dutch and a former ladies' golf champion. They have four boys, the eldest, Edward Charles, is named after his royal godfather. Van Cutsem farms and manages his own stud near Newmarket. Prince Charles often stays there, and is invariably included in the annual shoot.

More than one of Prince Charles's men-friends has married a former girlfriend of his. The Hon. Mark Vestey, who married Rose Clifton in 1975, is the brother of millionaire Lord (Sam) Vestey, chairman of Union International, which includes the Blue Star shipping-line, the Dewhurst chain of butchers' shops and large interests in South America. Both Vesteys are polo-players and run their own polo teams.

Another polo friend to win the friendship and full confidence of the Prince is an Australian, Sinclair Hill, a married man in his forties. The Prince of Wales has often stayed with him at his home in New South Wales, most recently during his official tour of Australia and New Zealand last April.

The Hon. Nicholas Soames is a larger than life character, in body as well as *bonhomie*, and is one of the few 'chums' that remain of the Prince's early friendships. The eldest son of Lord Soames – the former British Ambassador to Paris and later to the EEC – and Mary, third daughter of Sir Winston Churchill. When he left Eton, he went to Mons Officer Cadet School and was commissioned in the 11th Hussars, Prince Albert's Own. He has always been close to the Royal Family and was Princess Anne's escort at the Investiture of the Prince of Wales in July 1969. Later that year she attended a ball at the British Embassy in Paris given for him and his sister, Emma. He was appointed an Extra Equerry to Prince Charles in 1970 and accompanied the Prince when he represented the Queen at Fiji's independence celebrations in October 1974. He settled on stockbroking as a career. Recently, his services were required as an escort for Lady Diana while Prince Charles was away on his Antipodean tour. At his marriage to Catherine Weatherall on 4 June 1981, the Queen Mother, Princess Margaret and Lady Diana were the principal guests and the best man was Prince Charles.

Another close and long-standing friend is a cousin of the Prince, the Hon. Norton Knatchbull, who became Lord Romsey after the assassination of his grandfather, Lord Mountbatten. After Gordonstoun, Norton Knatchbull read politics at the University of Kent. He then went into the film industry (his father, Lord Brabourne, is one of Britain's leading film producers) and he worked on Zeffirelli's film *Romeo and Juliet* in Rome in 1967. He is now an associate producer for Thames Television. Lord Romsey and Prince Charles share a common interest in flying and farming. In 1975 the press tried to make something of their sightings of Prince Charles with Norton Knatchbull's established girlfriend, Penelope Eastwood. She became engaged to Norton Knatchbull in 1977. Their wedding was postponed when Lord Mountbatten and Norton's young brother, Nicholas, were assassinated in a bomb explosion on the family's boat. But on 4 December 1979 the marriage took place in Romsey Abbey in Hampshire and Prince Charles was his cousin's best man.

The Prince of Wales has several friends among his personal staff and in the Royal Household. His private secretary, the Hon. Edward Adeane, was the Prince's own appointment. He comes from a family dedicated over the last hundred years to the service of the monarch; his father, Sir Michael, now Lord Adeane, was for many years principal private secretary to the Queen. Edward Adeane, a bachelor in his early forties, gave up a lucrative practice as a libel lawyer to replace Squadron Leader Checketts, who had been the Prince's secretary for nine years.

Prince Philip, Prince Charles and Penelope Eastwood at Windsor in July 1975

Prince Charles and Lord Romsey. The Prince was best man to Lord Romsey at his wedding in December 1979.

Inevitably, those closest to the Prince are the men who spend the most time with him. These are the police officers from Special Branch (wrongly called detectives), who protect him and guard his interests. There are always two of them, one being on duty all the time, and they are both Chief Inspectors. John MacLean is a stocky Scot, while Paul Officer is tall and English. He was the man who overpowered the mentally unstable Royal Navy lieutenant who attacked the Prince one night when he was attending a course on underwater warfare at Portland, Dorset. Both policemen have been with the Prince for years, although 'Officer Officer' is leaving his service later this year after the wedding on his promotion to Superintendent.

Anthony George Merrick, 3rd Baron Tryon, is probably one of Prince Charles's most valued friends. Anthony was a Page of Honour to the Queen between January 1954 and November 1956 and stayed at Balmoral during the Queen's visits there. Over the last twenty years he has become a close friend of Prince Charles, despite the eight-year difference in their ages. They share a common passion for salmon-fishing and shooting. Lord Tryon and his Australian wife, Dale, often provide another 'safe house' for the Prince to stay in at weekends, from which to go out hunting, shooting or fishing.

About twenty-four years ago, during a summer holiday from Eton, Lord Tryon asked a friend of his to stay with his family at Balmoral. This friend was Timothy Tollemache, who was to become another friend of the Prince. Since that initial meeting, Tim Tollemache (pronounced 'Tolmash'), the 5th Baron, has worked with and become friends with other members of the Royal Family. After a short service commission in the Coldstream Guards, he was a pupil at Sandringham of the Queen's former land agent, Sir William Fellowes, father of Robert Fellowes, Lady Diana's brother-in-law. Lord Tollemache is now a director of the family firm, Tollemache and Cobbold Breweries. In 1970 he married Alexandra, daughter of the late Colonel Hugo Meynell, MC, a Derbyshire landowner. The Prince of Wales attended the wedding; Anthony Tryon was best man; and Lady Diana's brother, Charles Spencer, then aged four, was a page. Lord Tollemache succeeded to the title on the death of his father in 1975, inheriting the family homes of Helmingham Hall, near Stowmarket in Suffolk and Peckforton Castle near Tarporley in Cheshire. Prince Charles has often spent weekends with the Tollemaches, and it was through Lady Tollemache's encouragement that he first began riding in cross-country events.

Prince Charles with his personal bodyguard, Chief Inspector John Maclean, after the Prince had won a bottle of champagne at a polo match at Ham

Nearly all of Prince Charles's men-friends are older than himself. Some, indeed, to whom he looks for advice and stimulating intellectual argument, are of his parents' generation: men like Lord Butler, former Conservative Cabinet minister and a Master of Trinity College, Cambridge; and Sir John Miller, a Crown Equerry, who tutored the Prince in the joys of hunting. His parents' friend, Ronald Ferguson, is now his polo manager. Ferguson, a former major in the Life Guards, finds in his royal pupil 'all the characteristics I would like to see in a son. He is an extremely human person; he's sympathetic and charming, with nevertheless all the guts in the world. In my opinion he will make in due course a marvellous head of state.'

Besides the great fondness and respect he feels and shows for his parents and his grandmother, Prince Charles has always been very fond of his aunt, Princess Margaret, Countess of Snowdon. Since the break-up of her marriage to Lord Snowdon, the Prince has remained on excellent terms with both of them. As Constable of Caernarvon Castle, the Earl of Snowdon was the overseer of the Investiture of the Prince of Wales. Now a prize-winning television documentary-maker and an internationally acclaimed photographer, Snowdon was commissioned to take the official photographs of the engagement.

Of Prince Charles's girlfriends much has already been written and imagined, and both he and they have at times been harried and hunted beyond endurance by reporters and photographers. But neither he nor they were able to make more than formal protests and take no action other than that of uncharacteristic evasion, deception and denial. The girls were fair game from the newspapers' point of view and more vulnerable. For, as Prince Charles said: 'It's very hard on them. I have layers to protect me, but they are not used to it. It tends, sometimes, to put the really nice ones off.'

He was not yet twenty-one when in June 1969 he was interviewed on television and asked about the girl he would marry. He said: 'This is awfully difficult, because you have got to remember that when you marry in my position you are going to marry someone who, perhaps, is one day going to be Queen. You've got to choose somebody very carefully, I think, who could fulfil this particular role, and it has got to be somebody pretty unusual. The one advantage about marrying a princess, for instance, or somebody from a royal family, is that they do know what happens. The only trouble is that I often feel I'd like to marry somebody English, or, perhaps Welsh. Well, British anyway.'

For the next twelve years the press speculated rabidly about who that 'somebody pretty unusual' would be, and when the announcement of his choice was finally made, it was with both a sense of relief and a sigh in many quarters. But a hundred mothers and more must have had their dynastic ambitions for their daughters dashed by the news of the Prince's engagement. He was, after all, the most eligible bachelor in Britain, as well as one of the richest, and his future wife – who would become Princess of Wales, Duchess of Cornwall, Duchess of Rothesay, Countess of Chester, Countess of Carrick, Baroness of Renfrew, and Lady of the Isles – might well one day expect to be Queen. No mother could have hoped more for her daughter, or wished more for herself than that she might one day be the mother of a Queen, and indeed the fond grandmother of a future King.

No one was more concerned about Prince Charles's future wife than his own mother; he had to marry. There was no question of 'ought' or 'might'; it was 'must'. Nor could heart rule head without a thought – although twice in recent years other members of the Royal Family have been allowed to marry quite freely, such as Princess Anne and Prince Richard of Gloucester. Prince Charles's choice, although ultimately his own, was perforce in part determined by many subtle pressures and considerations, national and political as well as social, and for a man already inhibited to a degree by his own nature and position, it was never easy for him to meet or treat any girl with total naturalness or ease. Deeply conscious of his role as Prince and future King, he could not help but regard some of those girls who came his way as contenders for the role of Queen. He once said: 'I've fallen in love with all sorts of girls and I fully intend to go on doing so. But I've made sure I haven't married the first person I've fallen in love with . . . My marriage has to be for ever.'

Even before he reached his teens, official eyes had viewed with cautious appraisal or considered approval such candidates for his kingly hand as Princess Anne-Marie of Denmark and Princess Marie-Christina of the Netherlands, to name but two.

In the traditionalist eyes of the Palace, it was felt a Prince of Wales should marry a princess. But princesses were and are rare birds in democratized Europe, and even if the girls were suitable, their families were often not. The Prince of Wales, however, could not be expected to consort exclusively with ladies of the aristocracy. Bubbly blondes, whom he seemed to favour – fair-haired, well-formed and jolly nymphs – fizzed around him at the pop of a cork. The Palace, made nervous more than once by aspiring, amorous acquaintances of the Prince, must have slept uneasily in their own beds when he wined and dined ladies who were strictly speaking not 'ladies' – especially those who were American and/or actresses. But in twelve years the Prince never let the Palace down. His sense of propriety, decency and duty kept him from doing anything imprudent, without letting him be quite deprived. For inevitably he had every man's response to every woman – especially if he were a chauvinist sportsman – that the pretty, mysterious creatures could be fun, could be chased and caught and were fine to have around, although not best suited to a man's world and best understood and employed as a mother and wife. He knew his place, and expected any girlfriend or potential Princess of Wales to know and remember hers.

The first so-called girl in his life to teach him about the pitfalls of confidences was Rosaleen Bagge, daughter of Sir John Bagge, a retired major and landowner living near King's Lynn in Norfolk. While still at Gordonstoun and when holidaying at Sandringham he met her at a local dance; he was seventeen. Soon afterwards, in January 1966, he flew out to Australia and Timbertop. She wrote to him, and he replied. They exchanged several letters, and that was more or less that – until she spoke incautiously (she was only eighteen) to the *Daily Express* in May 1966. Asked about her first meeting with the schoolboy prince, she said: 'It was a snowball dance, where couples split up and pick other partners. He was standing in a corner by himself looking quite miserable. He was so terribly shy. . . . I'm not sure when I'll be writing again to Charles. Anyway, I think he owes *me* a letter!'

Her frankness to the press was fearfully penalized in royalist Norfolk, where Rosie Bagge was regarded for a time as if she were Mata Hari and Delilah combined. But the former model and freelance cook soon recovered and married a Norfolk neighbour, Captain Jonathan Buxton, of the 17th/21st Lancers.

Prince Charles's first serious friendship was with Lucia Santa Cruz, the dark-haired, twenty-three-year-old daughter of the Chilean ambassador. He was then twenty. They met in Cambridge. She was a research assistant to Lord Butler, the Master of Trinity College, where Prince Charles was an undergraduate. She often accompanied him on social outings in Cambridge and elsewhere, and was his guest at the party after his Investiture at Caernarvon. An accomplished linguist, she once told a reporter who inquired about the association: 'I no longer speak English.'

Lady Leonora Grosvenor, daughter of the Duke of Westminster, was the next noble girl to fire press speculation. Lady Leonora later married the photographer, Patrick, Earl of Lichfield. Her sister, Lady Jane, another friend of the Prince, is now the Duchess of Roxburghe.

There was also Tricia Nixon. But not even the press could take seriously President Nixon's blatant attempts to interest Prince Charles in his youngest daughter. This happened during a royal visit to Washington in July 1970. The Prince was not amused, and later described the luckless Tricia as 'plastic and artificial'.

A much more likely and as it proved actual romance was that between Prince Charles and Lady Jane Wellesley, only daughter of the 8th Duke of Wellington, who with his wife is an old friend of the Queen. He took Lady Jane to the Royal Tournament in July 1972, and for four years she was his frequent companion to the theatre, at dinner-parties and on holiday, most notably in Spain on her family's estate. She also stayed at Sandringham, attending a New Year's Party in 1973. Eventually she found it difficult to cope with press attention, her bright 'We're just good chums' becoming in time 'I'm fed up with all these rumours!' She was also determined to pursue her own career and is now working for Granada Television.

The high-spirited girls whom Prince Charles favoured must have sometimes found their public appearances none too easy. They had to call him 'Sir' and be content with playing second fiddle. He led the way – they walked behind. It was difficult to be entirely natural, having to be wary of what they said and did. He himself was slightly self-conscious, although he concealed this and his impenetrable reserve with a merry and joking manner. He was charming, but at the same time cavalier and diffident. He was also often away, not only on royal engagements but pursuing his service and sporting activities. No proper courtship was ever possible.

It was easier for him to consort with girls who were friends of friends, or party-girls and little more, at dinners or at other official functions – girls like film actress, Susan George, who was one of his 350 guests at his thirtieth birthday party at Buckingham Palace in November 1978; like Laura Jo Watkins, blonde, bubbly daughter of an American admiral whom he met at a yacht club in California – she later flew to London to hear him give his maiden speech in the House of Lords; like Helga Wagner, who had also attracted Edward Kennedy; and the daughter of landowner, Lord Manton, Fiona Watson.

Other girls, who appeared with him at polo-fields, at parties, in theatres and on holidays, were Lady Charlotte Manners, daughter of the Duke of Rutland;

Lady Jane Wellesley was a frequent companion of Prince Charles over a period of four years.

Left: Sabrina Guinness with Prince Charles at Cowdray Park in 1978

Right: Prince Charles and Lady Sarah Spencer with friends at Smith's Lawn, Windsor, on 24 July 1977

Libby Manners, the Duke of Rutland's niece, who stayed at Balmoral in 1978; Sabrina Guinness, who was once nanny to Ryan O'Neal's daughter, Tatum, in California, girl friday to David Bowie and is the daughter of merchant banker, Mr James Guinness; Amanda Knatchbull, grand-daughter of Earl Mountbatten; and Lady Sarah Spencer, elder sister of Lady Diana, who boldly said after a skiing holiday in the Prince's party in February 1978: 'Charles is a fabulous person – but I am not in love with him . . . I would not marry a man I did not love, whether it was a dustman or the King of England. If he asked me I would turn him down.' She always called him 'Sir'. 'I don't know what made me do this in the first place. It just seemed natural and I have done so ever since. It is obviously right to do so because I have never been corrected.'

There were many other girlfriends who were not as close to the Prince as the press made out. There was Jane Ward, aged twenty-three and divorced wife of Captain Toby Ward of the Royal Hussars. She was assistant manager of the Guards Polo Club at Windsor. She was quoted in July 1979 as saying: 'Prince Charles and I both know that . . . nothing could come of our friendship as I am a divorcee . . . he relaxes in my company because I don't treat him as untouchable . . . He knows we could never be married.' Mrs Ward, who happened to be watching the Prince play polo at Windsor the day her remarks appeared in a national paper, was spoken to by Chief Inspector Maclean, his police bodyguard, and left the field. She said sadly: 'I may never see him again.'

Press interest in Prince Charles's girlfriends increased as his thirtieth birthday in November 1978, neared and passed. For he had once said: 'The right age for marriage is around thirty. By this time you have seen a great deal of life, met a large number of girls, been able to see what types of girls there are, fallen in love every now and then, and you know what it's all about.'

The most avid speculation in the newspapers centred for a time towards the end of 1976 around Princess Marie-Astrid of Luxembourg. It was rumoured that the Queen, after a state visit to Luxembourg, had been favourably impressed by the Princess, daughter of the Grand Duke and a trained nurse. Prince Charles was not so taken with her or with the idea of marrying her. She was not, in fact, an ideal choice as she was a Roman Catholic. 'If I marry a Catholic,' he said, 'I'm dead.' In July 1980, the *Daily Express* published the headline: 'Charles to marry Astrid. Official.' The Queen's press secretary, Ronald Allison (now Controller, Sport and Outside Broadcasts at Thames Television), was instructed by Prince Charles to issue a denial. He said: 'They are not getting engaged this Monday, next Monday, the Monday after or any other Monday, Tuesday, Wednesday or Thursday. They do not know each other, and people who do not know each other do not get engaged. The Royal Family does not go in for arranged marriages.'

Not that the Prince of Wales would ever have married merely for reasons of state. He once said: 'If I'm deciding on whom I want to live with for the next fifty years – well, that's the last decision in which I'd want my head to be ruled entirely by my heart. It has nothing to do with class – it's to do with compatibility.'

His heart was in fact probably most engaged by three girls in the last ten years of his bachelorhood – Lady Jane Wellesley, Davina Sheffield, and Anna Wallace.

Davina Sheffield, the tall and lovely daughter of company director, George Sheffield, who died in 1968, was the grand-daughter of the first Lord McGowan and of Sir Berkely Sheffield, one of whose ancestors sold Buckingham House to George III. She is related to the Duke of Beaufort. In the early part of 1974 she had meningitis. Over a period of two years, from 1974 to 1976, she was the Prince of Wales' most regular companion. They met at a dinner party given by Lady Jane Wellesley. In August 1974 Davina was his guest at Balmoral. Then the *Daily Mail* revealed that she had been on holiday in the South of France with an Old Harrovian, James Beard, aged thirty, with whom she was said to be in love. Later they were said to be unofficially engaged. Soon afterwards, Davina disappeared from the public eye. In March 1975, after the craftshop she ran in Kensington began to fail, she went to Vietnam, where for five weeks she helped to care for some Vietnamese orphans in Saigon. After the fall of Saigon, she went to Bangkok, and on to Australia. Then, early in 1976, her widowed mother, Mrs Agnes Sheffield, was murdered by two youths who had broken into the family home at Ramsden in Oxfordshire; they were sentenced to life imprisonment. In the summer, Davina was once more seen in the company of the Prince, in Windsor Park and in Devon, when he was on shore-leave from HMS *Bronington*. In September the press suddenly seized on her as the Prince's *fiancée*-to-be and future queen. Mr Beard now revealed that he and Davina had once spent several months in a cottage near Winchester: 'I was very much in love with her,' he said. 'And we were both very happy.' He added: 'I think she will make an extremely good queen and a magnificent wife.' Davina also spoke out: 'I have seen reports in the newspapers about the Prince and myself, but there is nothing I can say.' She failed, however, to deny the rumour of an impending engagement and said, when asked about it: 'It is a private matter to me – although I have no doubt that people might regard it as public.' She flew to Scotland, to a Hebridean island where the press soon found her. She fled back to London, where at Heathrow Airport she was hounded by newspapermen into a ladies' lavatory. So Davina's royal romance came to an end and she faded from view. She now lives with her sister, is still single, and works in an art gallery in Kensington.

Another romance ended as suddenly. In September 1979, Prince Charles became friendly with Anna Wallace, the daughter of a Scottish landowner. He met her hunting with the Belvoir. But the association abruptly ended when in June 1980, during Ascot week, at a ball in Windsor Castle celebrating the Queen Mother's eightieth birthday, Miss Wallace, aged twenty-five, was sufficiently displeased by the Prince's dutiful attention to his social obligations that she left the castle in a fury, after saying somewhat forcibly and in public: 'Don't ever ignore me like that again! I've never been treated so badly in my life! And nobody – not even you – behaves that way to me!' It seems that Prince Charles was more upset by this *contretemps* than she, and tried to repair the breach – seeing her not long afterwards, at a a polo match and dance at Cirencester. But the lady was not for turning, disliking the Prince's third party approach (via police bodyguards and his staff), and

Davina Sheffield at a cross country team event. She was once a close companion of Prince Charles.

Left: Anna Wallace married the Hon. John Hesketh a few months after ending her relationship with Prince Charles in June 1980.

Right: Captain Andrew Parker-Bowles and Camilla Shand married at the Guards' Chapel on 4 July 1973.

married the Hon. John Fermor Hesketh, the younger brother of the former motor-racing millionaire, Lord Hesketh, a few months later.

By then, however, Lady Diana Spencer had been invited to spend a weekend at Balmoral as guest of the Prince of Wales.

Two of his closest women friends, outside his own family, are both married: Mrs Camilla Parker-Bowles and Lady Dale Tryon, at whose country-houses, both in Wiltshire, he has often stayed as a guest, able to relax in the uncritical, undemanding company of loyal and trusted friends.

Mrs Camilla Parker-Bowles is married to Lieutenant Colonel Andrew Parker-Bowles, and is the daughter of Major Bruce Shand, MC, and the Hon. Mrs Shand, sister of the present Lord Ashcombe, who is the former chairman of the construction firm, Holland, Hammond and Cubitt. She was a close companion of Prince Charles while Andrew Parker-Bowles squired Princess Anne. The ensuing friendship of Camilla and Andrew resulted in their marriage at the Guards' Chapel in July 1973. Among the 800 guests were the Queen Mother, Princess Margaret and Princess Anne. Their country home is a mile northwest of Chippenham in Wiltshire. They have two children, Prince Charles's godson, Thomas, who is nearly six, and Laura, aged three. Lieutenant Colonel Parker-Bowles commanded the Sovereign's Escort at the Royal Wedding and the Prince of Wales' Escort when he and the Princess of Wales left Buckingham Palace for their honeymoon.

Lady Tryon is an Australian and nine months older than Prince Charles. As Dale Elizabeth Harper, elder daughter of a wealthy and successful Melbourne publisher, Barry Harper, she went to school at Lauriston and then to a finishing school, Invergowrie. After this she worked for a time for the Australian national airline, Qantas, in the public relations department, before becoming the fashion writer in Melbourne of *The Australian Woman's Weekly*, a position she held for three years. In December 1971 she came to England, staying with friends and writing the occasional fashion article for Australian consumption.

At a dinner party given for her by the young Earl of Shelburne to celebrate her twenty-fourth birthday on 3 January 1972, she met her future husband, the Hon. Anthony Tryon, a company director in the City and then in his early thirties. She had invited her sister over from Paris to join in the celebrations, and the Earl asked his Wiltshire neighbour, Anthony Tryon, to make up the numbers. He and Dale Harper became engaged in the autumn of that year. A tall, dark, handsomely aristocratic man with an engaging smile and manner, he was educated at Eton, and instead of going to Sandhurst like most of his friends, he opted to go to Australia, where he spent a year (1959–60) in Queensland 'jackarooing', working as a cowboy on a cattle-station. On his return to England he joined the merchant bankers, Lazard's (he is now a director), and was sent a year or so later to their office in Melbourne. He is a director of several companies, apart from Lazard's, and including the gunsmiths patronized by Prince Charles, Purdey & Sons.

Lady Tryon met Prince Charles in 1970 through her husband, who has known the Prince since he was a boy – Anthony's father was part of the Queen's Household as Keeper of the Privy Purse, and Deputy Senior Steward of the Jockey Club. When Dale returned to Melbourne in November 1977, her father, who had not seen her for over three years, gave a large party for her at which Prince Charles, who was in Australia on an official visit, was a guest.

Anthony Tryon and Dale Harper were married on Friday, 13 April 1973 in the Chapel Royal, St James's Palace. The best man was the Earl of Pembroke, and Princess Margaret and Prince Michael of Kent were the chief guests. The honeymoon was spent on the Island of Mustique in Princess Margaret's house, Jolies Eaux. The Tryons have four children, the last two being twins, a boy and a girl. Prince Charles is godfather to their second child, a boy born in May 1976 and christened Charles.

In 1976, the 2nd Baron Tryon, Anthony's father, died at the age of seventy, and Anthony succeeded to the title as the 3rd Baron and moved with his wife and first two children into Ogbury House, on a 1200-acre Wiltshire estate near the village of Great Durnford.

Ogbury House, Wiltshire, home of Lord and Lady Tryon

Lady Dale Tryon loves her house in the country – there is another home in Walton Street, London – and takes great pains when entertaining to ensure that everything about her home is pleasing to the eye and a pleasure for her guests. An attractive, vivacious woman, she is both a romantic and a realist, warm-hearted and perceptive, open-minded yet most discreet. In no way a snob, she still retains her native Australian accent (which prompts Prince Charles to call her Kanga). She is an excellent hostess. Weekend hunting and shooting parties at Ogbury House are cheerfully informal affairs, with an emphasis on good food and enjoyment. 'We try and live off the land in Wiltshire. That means salmon, trout, venison, partridge, pheasant, woodcock and snipe.'

Prince Charles is a great friend of the Tryons. Every August, since 1975, he has holidayed with them in Iceland, taking time off from his Balmoral holiday to enjoy a week or more with the Tryons and one or two other friends, such as his secretary, Edward Adeane, fishing for salmon in the rivers of northeast Iceland. They stay in a small lodge that can sleep ten, situated by the River Hofsá near Vopnafjördur.

Now that the Prince and Princess of Wales are married it remains to be seen which of all their friends will continue to be close friends of both. It will also be interesting to see who become their new friends.

Left: Lady Dale Tryon

CHAPTER 6

The Families' Weddings

Although royal weddings have normally been held in Westminster Abbey in the twentieth century, the convention is very much a modern one, stemming from the marriage in February 1919 of Princess Patricia of Connaught (one of Queen Victoria's many grand-daughters) to Sir Alexander Ramsay. Until then, for over seven hundred years, not a single member of a reigning monarch's family had been married in the Abbey – the last such wedding before Princess Patricia's was that of Edmund, Earl of Lancaster, in 1270. Although Richard II married in Westminster in 1383, it is not clear whether the wedding took place in the Abbey or the Palace.

For centuries, the weddings of British kings and queens and their children had been very private affairs, usually conducted in royal chapels, and occasionally on the Continent. There was no particularly favoured place, although the chapels in St James's Palace and Windsor Castle were much used. Royal weddings were very informal occasions, despite the reasons of state and policy that brought the often ill-suited couples together.

When Princess Mary, the eldest daughter of the Duke of York (later James II, who produced no legitimate male heir) was married to Prince William of Orange on Sunday, 4 November 1677, the sixteen-year-old bride was in tears and the bridegroom, aged twenty-seven, seemed depressed. Cheerfulness was only attempted by the bride's uncle, Charles II, who contributed a string of coarse pleasantries, and finally urged Prince William, as he sat with his young wife on the marriage-bed after receiving the congratulations of the assembled royals and senior ministers and clergy: 'Now, nephew, to your work! Hey! St George for England!'

It is said of the wedding night of the future George IV and Princess Caroline of Brunswick in April 1795 that no Prince of Wales or king ever approached the marriage-bed with such antipathy – not since the wedding of Henry VIII and Anne of Cleves. The odour and appearance of his bride offended his sensibilities so much that he could not endure her company unless fortified with brandy, and it is indeed alleged that he failed altogether to ascend the bed and spent the night in a drunken stupor on the floor, where his determined bride consummated their union.

Propriety on these royal occasions, as well as dignity and love, date from the marriage of Queen Victoria to Prince Albert, which she described in her journal for Monday, 10 February 1840:

Got up at a ¼ to 9 – Well, and having slept well; and breakfasted at ½ p. 9. Mamma came before and brought me a nosegay of orange flowers . . . Had my hair dressed and the wreath of orange flowers put on. Saw Albert for the *last* time *alone*, as my *Bridegroom*. Dressed . . . At ½ p. 12 I set off, dearest Albert having gone before. I wore a white satin gown with a very deep flounce of Honiton lace, imitation of old. I wore my Turkish diamond necklace and earrings, and Albert's beautiful sapphire brooch. Mamma and the Duchess of Sutherland went in the carriage with me. I never saw such crowds of people as there were in the Park, and they cheered most enthusiastically. When I arrived at St James's, I went into the dressing-room where my 12 young Train-bearers were, dressed all in white with white roses, which had a beautiful effect. Here I waited a little till dearest Albert's Procession had moved into the Chapel. I then went with my Train-bearers and ladies into the Throne-room, where the Procession formed . . . [It] looked beautiful going downstairs . . . The Flourish of Trumpets ceased as I entered the Chapel, and the organ began to play, which had a beautiful effect. At the Altar, to my right, stood Albert; Mamma was on my left as also the Dukes of Sussex and Cambridge, and Aunt Augusta . . . Lord Melbourne stood close to me with the Sword of State. The Ceremony was very imposing, and fine and simple, and I think *ought* to make an ever-lasting impression on every one who promises at the Altar to *keep* what he or she promises. Dearest Albert repeated everything very distinctly. I felt so happy when the ring was put on, and by Albert. As soon as the Service was over, the Procession returned as it came, with the exception that my beloved Albert led me out. The

The wedding of Princess Anne and Captain Mark Phillips on 14 November 1973 – the last royal wedding in Westminster Abbey

applause was very great . . . Lord Melbourne, a good man, was very much affected during the Ceremony and at the applause. We all returned to the Throne-room, where the Signing of the Register took place . . . I then returned to Buckingham Palace alone with Albert; they cheered us really most warmly and heartily; the crowd was immense; and the Hall at Buckingham Palace was full of people; they cheered us again and again. The great Drawing-room and Throne-room were full of people of rank, and numbers of children were there . . . I went and sat on the sofa in my dressing-room with Albert; and we talked together there from 10 m. to 2 till 20 m. p. 2. Then we went downstairs where all the Company was assembled and went into the dining-room – dearest Albert leading me in.

I sat between dearest Albert and the Duke of Sussex. My health and dearest Albert's were drunk . . . Albert and I drank a glass of wine with Lord Melbourne, who seemed much affected by the whole . . . I went upstairs and undressed and put on a white silk gown trimmed with swansdown, and a bonnet with orange flowers. Albert went downstairs and undressed. At 20 m. to 4 Lord Melbourne came to me and stayed with me till 10 m. to 4. I shook hands with him and he kissed my hand . . . 'Nothing could have gone off better,' he said . . . I pressed his hand once more, and he said, 'God bless you, Ma'am,' most kindly, and with such a kind look. Dearest Albert came up and fetched me downstairs, where we took leave of Mamma and drove off at near 4; I and Albert alone.

Queen Victoria had twelve bridesmaids to carry her train, which was eighteen feet long. In this she established a record and a precedent – bridesmaids

Left: The wedding of Queen Victoria and Prince Albert at the Chapel Royal, St James's Palace, 10 February 1840, by Sir George Hayter

Right: Princess Mary, daughter of George V and Queen Mary, married Viscount Lascelles in 1922.

Below: Lady Elizabeth Bowes-Lyon (now Queen Elizabeth the Queen Mother) leaving her home for her wedding to the Duke of York, second son of George V, in Westminster Abbey on 26 April 1923.

becoming a necessary adjunct to a wedding ever since. She was also the first English bride to wear her veil off her face during the marriage ceremony. Princess Patricia, her grand-daughter and daughter of the Duke of Connaught and Strathearn, had eight bridesmaids at her wedding in 1919 – as did Princess Mary, another grand-daughter of Queen Victoria, who in 1922 married Viscount Lascelles (later the 6th Earl of Harewood). Princess Mary, later the Princess Royal, was the eldest daughter of George V and Queen Mary, who married in July 1893 as the Duke and Duchess of York. The bride was attended by ten bridesmaids, all princesses, one being Princess Alice of Battenberg, the future mother of Prince Philip.

At the marriage of Princess Mary in 1922, one of the bridesmaids was a daughter of the Earl of Strathmore, Lady Elizabeth Bowes-Lyon (now Queen Elizabeth the Queen Mother). She herself was married in the Abbey, with eight bridesmaids, the following year to the Duke of York, who was the second son of George V. Lady Elizabeth virtually designed her own wedding-dress, taking her ideas to Handley Seymour who created the final design. It was a dress of ivory chiffon moiré in a simple, slender medieval style with a square neckline and dropped waistline; the centre panel was embroidered in silver thread, pearls and beads and inset with silver *lamé*. Her short train was edged with old *point de Flandres*

Princess Marina of Greece married Prince George, Duke of Kent, and fourth son of George V, on 29 November 1934 in Westminster Abbey.

lace, lent by Queen Mary. Thirteen years later, in December 1936, the Duke and Duchess of York became King and Queen on the abdication of King Edward VIII.

Their first child, a girl, was born a fortnight after Easter in April 1926, at 17 Bruton Street, off Berkeley Square, in the London home (now Lombards Bank) of the Earl and Countess of Strathmore, the parents of the Duchess of York. The infant princess, born at 2.40 a.m. on Wednesday, 21 April, was christened Elizabeth Alexandra Mary. The likelihood at the time of her becoming Queen was remote: her parents could expect to have a son, and her uncle, David, Prince of Wales, was expected to marry and have children, sons, of his own.

The Duke of York wrote to his mother, Queen Mary: 'You don't know what a tremendous joy it is to Elizabeth and me to have our little girl. We always wanted a child to make our happiness complete, and now that it has at last happened, it seems so wonderful and strange . . . I do hope that you and Papa are as delighted as we are, to have a grand-daughter, or would you have sooner had another grandson? I know Elizabeth wanted a daughter.' In a letter to his father, George V, the Duke of York wrote: 'I hope you will approve of her names, and I am sure there will be no muddle over two Elizabeths in the family. We are so anxious for her first name to be Elizabeth, as it is such a nice name, and there has been no one of that name in your family for such a long time . . .' In fact it had been four hundred years, in the autumn of 1533, since Elizabeth I was born. *Her* grandparents were Elizabeth of York and Henry VII; her father was Henry VIII and her mother, Anne Boleyn.

Princess Elizabeth, at the age of eight, was one of the eight bridesmaids at the Abbey wedding in 1934 of Princess Marina of Greece and Prince George, the Duke of Kent and fourth son of George V and Queen Mary. Princess Marina's slim, sophisticated dress, designed by Edward Molyneux, was of supple *lamé*, with a flower design in silver and white brocade, and a train of Valenciennes lace. Three years earlier, Miss Ruth Gill, Lady Diana's grandmother, had worn a gown of ivory satin with a shawl of old lace at her wedding to Lord Fermoy in Aberdeen.

In 1935, the third son of George V and Queen Mary, Henry, Duke of Gloucester, married Lady Alice Montagu-Douglas-Scott. Princess Elizabeth, now aged nine, was again a bridesmaid, as was her younger sister, Princess Margaret. Lady Alice's father, however, died just before the wedding and the Abbey ceremony was cancelled. The Gloucesters were married eventually at Buckingham Palace, in the chapel that was later destroyed in World War II.

The wedding of Princess Elizabeth and Lieutenant Philip Mountbatten on 20 November 1947 was the first royal marriage since the war. Princess Margaret was one of the eight bridesmaids, and the two five-year-old page-boys were Prince Michael of Kent and Prince William of Gloucester, both dressed in kilts. Norman Hartnell designed the bride's dress. James Laver wrote: 'Mr Norman Hartnell has shown himself no mean poet. In a design based on delicate

Princess Elizabeth (now Queen Elizabeth II) married Lieutenant Philip Mountbatten on 20 November 1947.

Miss Ruth Gill (Lady Diana's grandmother) married Lord Fermoy in Aberdeen on 17 September 1931.

The Hon. Frances Roche (Lady Diana's mother), with her father, Lord Fermoy, leaving for her wedding to Viscount Althorp in Westminster Abbey on 1 June 1954.

Botticelli curves, he has scattered over the ivory satin garlands of white York roses carried out in raised pearls, entwined with ears of corn minutely embroidered in crystal. By the device of reverse embroidery he has alternated star flowers and orange blossom, now tulle on satin and now satin on tulle, the whole encrusted with pearls and crystals.' The silk came from nationalist China, and not from those countries who had recently been wartime enemies – Italy and Japan.

Lady Diana's mother, the Hon. Frances Roche, married Viscount Althorp at Westminster Abbey on 1 June 1954. Her dress was designed by Eva Lutyens: it was simple yet ornate, a full-skirted gown of white faille, embroidered on a close-fitting bodice, sleeves and skirt with diamanté, sequins and rhinestones. A diamond tiara belonging to her mother held the white tulle veil in place. Her bouquet was of lilies of the valley, white roses and stephanotis.

Princess Margaret chose a strikingly unadorned white dress for her marriage to Antony Armstrong-Jones in Westminster Abbey in May 1960. The dress, designed by Norman Hartnell, was made of white silk organza, piped with organza rouleau. The close-fitting bodice had long, tight sleeves with a V-neckline at the front. The full-flowing skirt had twelve panels, each joined with fine rouleau piping, and at the back it fanned out into a train. She carried

Princess Margaret wore a dress of silk organza at her wedding to Antony Armstrong-Jones in May 1960. Princess Anne (second from the right) was a bridesmaid.

a bouquet of orchids, lilies of the valley and stephanotis. Her eight bridesmaids were little girls, led by ten-year-old Princess Anne, who was a bridesmaid again the following year at the wedding in York Minster of the present Duke of Kent and Miss Katharine Worsley. John Cavanagh designed Miss Worsley's wedding-dress, which, along with those of her bridesmaids, used 273 yards of material. The small roll collar of the bodice of the wedding-dress stood well away from the neck, and the skirt gently belled at the front and flowed back into a double train.

When Princess Alexandra married the Hon. Angus Ogilvy in Westminster Abbey on 24 April 1963 she was attended by seven children. Her dress was also designed by John Cavanagh: it was made of fine cotton lace, tinted with magnolia. The simple bodice had a high round neckline and full-length sleeves, and the skirt flowed in an unbroken line, sweeping out at the back into a long train. Her veil, bordered by old Valenciennes lace, was kept in place by the diamond tiara that her mother, Princess Marina, had worn at her wedding in 1934.

Ten years later, on 14 November 1973 – Prince Charles's twenty-fifth birthday – the wedding of Princess Anne to Captain Mark Phillips marked what may well have been the end of seventy years of royal weddings in the Abbey. In a break with tradition, her dress, designed by Maureen Baker, was made by the ready-to-wear house of Susan Small. It had a high stand-up neckline, a tailored bodice and trumpet sleeves. The dress was trimmed with pearls

and beads. She broke another royal tradition (set by Queen Victoria) by wearing her veil over her face during the service. It was made of fine tulle, embroidered with flowers picked out in beads. Another twentieth-century precedent was broken by the bride, who dispensed with any bridesmaids – 'yards of uncontrollable children', as she said; she herself had been six times a bridesmaid. Instead, she had only two attendants, both aged nine: her cousin, Lady Sarah Armstrong-Jones, and her youngest brother, Prince Edward.

The changing style, place and manner of such formally grand occasions was signalled in July 1972 by the marriage of Prince Richard of Gloucester (the present Duke) and Miss Birgitte van Deurs, the daughter of a Danish lawyer. The ceremony took place in a village church at Barnwell in Northamptonshire and was very much a private family affair. In keeping with the simple wedding, the bride wore a white Swiss organdie dress, trimmed with lace, and a plain white veil. Her bouquet of flowers was prepared by Princess Alice, her mother-in-law.

Quite a different affair was the marriage of Prince Michael of Kent in June 1978 to Baroness Marie-Christine von Reibnitz. His bride was not only a divorcee but also a Roman Catholic, and they were married – after special permission was obtained and after Prince Michael had renounced his right of succession to the throne (he was sixteenth in line) – at a civil ceremony in the Town Hall in Vienna.

Lady Diana's sister, Lady Jane Spencer, married Robert Fellowes, the Queen's assistant private secretary in April 1978 at the Guards' Chapel in London. She wore a dress of cream silk georgette: the bodice and sleeves being of Victorian lace. The dress was designed by Bill Pashley. The Spencer tiara held her veil in place and she carried a bouquet of lilies of the valley, freesias and stephanotis.

Lady Diana's eldest sister, Lady Sarah, married Neil McCorquodale, a Lincolnshire landowner and former Coldstream Guards officer, on 17 May 1980 at St Mary's Church, Great Brington. It was the first wedding at Althorp since 1914, when Lady Delia married there. Lady Sarah wore a plain dress designed by Bill Pashley. It was embroidered with antique lace and georgette in the style of a riding-habit. Her veil, also trimmed with lace, was held in place by the Spencer tiara. Her bridesmaids included Lady Sarah Armstrong-Jones, the daughter of Princess Margaret and Lord Snowdon.

The wedding of Prince Charles and Lady Diana in St Paul's Cathedral paves the way for repetition or for further change. The younger members of the Royal Family may well surprise us by the churches and places chosen for their weddings. Indeed, the Abbey, apart from state occasions, may not see a royal wedding for many years. Its next great royal occasion may prove to be the coronation of Charles III.

In any event, no such royal wedding as that of the Prince of Wales and Lady Diana Spencer is likely to happen again in the twentieth century. It could well be the last of its kind, and the wedding of the next Prince of Wales, in thirty years or so from now, may be very different.

Opposite above: Lady Jane Spencer married Robert Fellowes on 20 April 1978. Lady Diana was a bridesmaid and is seen here in the back row.

Opposite below: Lady Sarah Spencer married Neil McCorquodale at St Mary's Church, Great Brington near Althorp on 17 May 1980. Lady Sarah Armstrong-Jones (in the back row) was a bridesmaid. Earl Spencer is seated on the left of the picture beside the groom's mother, with the Hon. Mrs Peter Shand Kydd and Mr Alistair McCorquodale to the right.

CHAPTER 7

The Houses of the Prince

Home for the royal couple will at first be a house in Gloucestershire, Highgrove House in the south Cotswolds, a square but pleasant Georgian mansion set in a small park beside the A433 and the hamlet of Doughton (pronounced 'Duffton'), about a mile southwest of Tetbury.

Tetbury is a compact and cosy little market town set on a low hill between the confluence of two streams, one being the headwaters of the River Avon. Largely untouched by the uglier developments of the nineteenth century, it retains an agreeable eighteenth-century simplicity and is now designated as a conservation area; the population numbers about 4,000. Its early fortunes were based on wool and agriculture; now its main industries are engineering and warehousing, and its nine pubs are outnumbered by antique shops. The town has seen three kings and two queens. During the Civil War, in August 1643, Charles I dined in Tetbury *en route* from Bristol to Gloucester. In 1663, Charles II passed through Tetbury with his queen on their way to Bath, as did James II in 1687 and Queen Anne in 1702. After that, nothing remotely royal occurred in Tetbury for over 270 years, until the birth in the town's Cotswold Hospital in 1949 of Mark Phillips, who would one day marry Princess Anne.

The town's main feature, and a landmark for miles, is the tall spire of the parish church of St Mary the Virgin. The original medieval church, having fallen into decay, was pulled down – apart from the fifteenth-century tower and spire – and rebuilt between 1777 and 1781 in 'an elegant and regular Gothic plan', with exceptionally large windows, slender columns, and a gallery around three sides. Kenneth Clark (Lord Clark) said of it: 'It is not devoid of a certain distinction, and is typical of ecclesiastical Gothic for the next fifty years.' For many years, after a violent thunderstorm, the spire leaned 4ft 6ins to the south. By 1891 it had become so dangerous that both spire and tower were taken down and rebuilt. The cost of this reconstruction, £10,000, was borne by a Mr Yatman who lived at Highgrove, the work being undertaken as a monument to and in memory of his son, Captain Hamilton Yatman. He liked to see the spire from the windows of his house and kept the view free of trees. Nowadays the spire is floodlit at night.

Highgrove House, Doughton

Highgrove

Highgrove House was built between 1796 and 1798 by a young lawyer, John Paul Paul, then in his mid-twenties, on an estate which had belonged to his maternal grandfather, Robert Clark. John Paul Paul's father, Josiah Paul Tippetts, had taken his maternal grandfather's surname, Paul, in 1787, on inheriting the lands of his uncle, John Paul of Tetbury. The young lawyer eventually became High Sheriff of Wiltshire in 1807, and bought the manor of Doughton in 1818. Highgrove passed on his death to his second son, Walter Paul. Prince Charles and John Paul Paul have a common sixteenth-century ancestor in Richard Pitt of Weymouth. Prince Charles is descended through the Queen Mother from Pitt's daughter, Grace, and John Paul Paul from her sister, Margaret.

The house was badly damaged by fire in 1893 and sold by the then owner, Mr Yatman, to a Colonel Mitchell, who rebuilt the southeast wing and the front. A number of eighteenth-century fireplaces were installed by the next owner, Colonel Morgan-Jones, in about 1950; he also enlarged the estate. In 1974, the house and grounds were purchased by the Conservative MP, the Rt. Hon. Maurice Macmillan. He seldom stayed there and the house was rented for two years to a retired brigadier general, James Roosevelt, son of the former American president.

Highgrove was put up for sale in 1980, the freehold of 348 acres being offered as a whole or in three lots, to be auctioned off (unless sold previously) at the Hare and Hounds, Westonbirt, at 3 p.m. on 30 July. Lot 1 consisted of 170 acres and included – apart from

Highgrove House itself – the Lodge Cottage, the Manager's House, two farm cottages, a stable block, a dairy unit and some farm buildings. Highgrove was described by the estate agents, Humberts, in their brochure, as 'a distinguished Georgian house with spacious but easily managed accommodation comprising 4 Reception Rooms, Domestic Quarters, 9 Bedrooms (5 with Dressing Room), 6 Bathrooms, Nursery Wing, full central heating and standing in well-timbered parkland.' It was rated at £934.

Four years before it came on the market, Princess Anne, who was then searching for a country house in the neighbourhood, was shown around Highgrove and was keen to buy it. When Lord Butler offered to sell her Gatcombe Park, situated between Tetbury and Stroud, she chose to buy Gatcombe instead of Highgrove. However, when in May 1980 she heard that Highgrove was up for sale she telephoned her elder brother. He bought the house and grounds, through the Duchy of Cornwall, for about £800,000, a price determined by its 348 acres rather than by the house itself.

At the time its suitability as a base for his various social and sporting activities and obligations must have made it seem a very desirable purchase. For one thing, London was a hundred miles away at the end of the M4 and Windsor even less: it would take just over an hour for the Prince to drive from Windsor Castle to Highgrove. Apart from the fact that the house is near his sister's home, in whose pursuits and interests he might share (although Lady Diana has no love for horses), another royal young couple, Prince and Princess Michael of Kent, also live in the neighbourhood, in Nether Lypiatt Manor, on the other side of Stroud. Perhaps more importantly, several of the Prince's loyal friends are in the area. Across the border with Wiltshire live Lieutenant Colonel Andrew Parker-Bowles and his wife Camilla, at Bolehyde Manor in Allington, and Lord and Lady Tryon are some 40 miles to the southeast, near Salisbury. The Duchy of Cornwall's estates in the West Country, including the Isles of Scilly, are also reasonably accessible for their owner's occasional inspections. There is polo in Cirencester Park, racing at Cheltenham, Newbury, Bath and Chepstow, the horse trials at Badminton, and the Beaufort Hunt, one of the leading packs of hounds in the country – Highgrove being in Monday and Saturday Country. In addition, the RAF station at Kemble, home of the Red Arrows, is conveniently close for royal trips around Britain, and the Principality of Wales is less than 30 miles away across the Severn Bridge. Finally, the cities of Gloucester, Bristol and Bath are almost equidistant from Highgrove itself.

Since its purchase by Prince Charles, the house has been extensively renovated, and the 'estate', once a mixed farm, is now down to grass. It presents a well-managed appearance, with neat fences and good Cotswold stone walls, with hunt-jumps in most fields.

Nonetheless, despite its attractions, Highgrove is a curious choice for the family home of the Prince of Wales. One can understand why Prince Charles should have relinquished his possession of Chevening House, near Sevenoaks in Kent, given along with its 3,500 acres by the 7th and last Earl Stanhope as a bequest to the nation in 1967, with the particular hope that it would be used by the Prince of Wales. The Regency mansion, with eighty-three rooms, might have seemed too large, too formal and impersonal, like the stately home it is. Presumably, despite its nearness to London – 20 miles south of the capital – it was also inconveniently situated, for a variety of sporting and social reasons, and not the kind of house, although it had been renovated at considerable cost, that would ever become a home. It was also very close to the M25 and a security nightmare. Yet Highgrove may ultimately prove to be just as unsatisfactory.

The house, to begin with, is an unexceptional residence for a future king, whose chosen domicile, if not palatial, could have been a place of much architectural merit as well as of great charm and beauty. To all outward appearances Highgrove is a plain, ivy-covered building, distinguished more by its lack of distinction than anything else. The house is approached by way of a new set of entrance gates made by local craftsmen to a design chosen by the Prince himself. These gates were presented by the town of Tetbury as a wedding present. A curved drive leads to the front of the house which faces north and east, with a view of parkland pasture, a ha-ha and trees and, through a gap in the trees, the A433 and the distant spire of Tetbury Church. The rooms at the rear, facing south and west, have an outlook curtailed by a thick copse and impeded by a darkly magnificent and spreading cedar of Lebanon, whose branches since the sale have been lopped. Before the sale a path, edged by yellow privets, square or domed, like playbricks, led from the rear of the house across a wide lawn lined by herbaceous borders, bushes and trees, to an oblong lily-pond. Wistaria, clematis and a magnolia grew up the sides of the house, which was entered at the front through a small, colonnaded porch and lobby. Beyond was a large oak-floored hall as wide as the house, with a heavy marble fireplace.

Right: Prince Charles and Lady Diana in Tetbury on 22 May 1981. The church spire can be seen in the background and the vicar of Tetbury, the Reverend Michael Sherwood, is on the right.

Overleaf: The gardens at Highgrove House; these have since been landscaped by Manning Roper.

The drawing room at Highgrove as it was when the house was owned by Maurice Macmillan

All the rooms at the time of the sale were plainly appointed but well-proportioned, the drawing-room on the southern wing being the largest, with eight big windows overlooking the lawn. Fireplaces and bookcases were a feature of most rooms on the ground floor, as were the old-fashioned grid-iron radiators which used to heat the house. On the first floor were four bedroom suites and the second floor was occupied by five more bedrooms and bathrooms.

The house has been redecorated and refurbished by a South-African-born interior designer, Dudley Poplak, furnishing the rooms with some of the Prince of Wales' favourite possessions and with some of the

Badminton House, home of the Duke of Beaufort. Prince Charles hunts with the Beaufort Hunt.

couple's wedding presents. The interior of the house has been decorated in accordance with the Princess of Wales' definite ideas on colour and design. Yet despite all this, with the general convenience of Highgrove's position and the undeniable pleasure the newly-weds feel about their own new home, some reservations about it must remain.

Highgrove House is still much exposed to public scrutiny, and accordingly not the kind of place, with its new bullet-proof glass, that may easily serve as a permanent royal home or a home for royal children. Several public rights of way traverse the grounds, and although young fast-growing trees have been planted between the house and the main road, car headlights on the A433 are in constant view from the front of the house at night.

It seems likely that the occupancy by Prince Charles and his young wife of Highgrove House will be temporary and their visits brief. Sooner rather than later, although he is very fond of the house, he may make his home in a country house more befitting his status and his pride in his wife, in a mansion more suitable for his children, and more safely protected from intrusion and the eyes of the curious.

It has been rumoured in the neighbourhood that a house such as Badminton House, eight miles to the south in the county of Avon, would be an ideal home. A fine, late seventeenth-century mansion, altered *circa* 1740 by William Kent, who gave it an attractive Palladian coating of ornamental pedestals and cupolas, it is overdue for a complete overhaul and repair, and could be made exceedingly attractive. The rooms have style, the public ones being impressive and ornate. It was in the entrance hall that the game of badminton was invented and evolved. The expansive park is the scene every April of the Three-Day Event Horse Trials, begun by the present Duke of Beaufort, now aged eighty-one, in 1949 and now televised by the BBC.

The Gloucestershire police guard *three* royal homes, and local ratepayers pay for half of the annual cost of the twenty-four-hour police watch on Gatcombe Park (£30,000), Nether Lypiatt (£20,000) and now Highgrove (£50,000). This burden would be lighter if the county had fewer royal homes.

The optimum solution would be the building of a completely new house. The last royal residence to be built as such was Sandringham, over a hundred years ago. Perhaps the Prince of Wales may one day put his seal on architectural history by the construction of a purpose-built modern royal home, perhaps on land in the Duchy of Cornwall, or in Wales, using the best designers, materials and craftsmen that Britain can provide.

Clarence House and Kensington Palace

Prince Charles spent nearly three years of his childhood in Clarence House, now the London home of the Queen Mother. In time she may well be pleased to relinquish her occupancy of the house and hand it over to her grandson and his young wife. But in the meantime, the official residence of the Prince and Princess of Wales will be in Kensington Palace.

The Palace has been a royal residence since 1689, when William III bought the original building on the site, Nottingham House, from the Earl of Nottingham. George I was the last king to live there, and it was in the reign of George III that the Palace

Clarence House, the London home of Queen Elizabeth the Queen Mother

Above: Buckingham Palace was often known as the Queen's House during the reign of George III. An aquatint by Thomas Rowlandson, 1809.

Opposite page: The White Drawing Room, Buckingham Palace. The Royal Family often use this room for assembling before a state function.

Buckingham Palace. Prince Charles's second-floor apartment overlooked The Mall and St James's Park.

buildings were divided into apartments for the Royal Family and grace and favour homes for the Household. Kensington Palace is now the home of Princess Margaret, as well as the London residence of the Duke and Duchess of Gloucester. Lady Jane Fellowes, Lady Diana's sister, lives with her husband in Palace apartments in the Old Barracks.

Apartments 8 and 9, which were badly damaged by incendiary bombs in World War II and remained derelict until 1975, have since been repaired and restored by the Department of the Environment, and once they have been fully decorated and furnished will be occupied by the Prince and Princess of Wales before the end of the year. The apartments consist of three reception rooms, a dining-room, a master bedroom suite, two guest bedrooms, a nursery suite and rooms for the staff.

Buckingham Palace

The Palace, at one end of The Mall, which divides St James's Park and Green Park, was originally called Buckingham House. It was built in 1703 as a red-brick mansion for John Sheffield, Duke of Buckingham and Normandy, having been designed by a Dutch architect. It was bought from Sir John Sheffield, the illegitimate son of the last Duke of Buckingham, in 1762 by George III, as a home for himself and his new Queen, away from the formalities, opulence and intrigues of the Court at St James's Palace. It cost George III £28,000, although he spent more on its alteration and redecoration. It was known then as the Queen's House, and at that time it was surrounded by parks and gardens, and meadows where cattle grazed. What is now the *inner* courtyard of Buckingham Palace was then the forecourt of the house. A major reconstruction in the Classic style was begun by George IV in 1825, the architect being John Nash. This was continued by William IV (1830–37) and Queen Victoria. A new wing was built in 1846 and the great ballroom ten years later. The present familiar façade is as recent as 1913 (as is the Victoria Memorial in front of the Palace), when the building was totally refronted in Portland stone and designed in a simple Renaissance style by Sir Aston Webb.

The Palace suffered some damage in World War II, in September 1940, when bombs dropped by a solitary German bomber on a daytime raid wrecked the

chapel, the swimming-pool and two pavilions. No one was hurt, although a few days later another stick of bombs, exploding in the forecourt and The Mall, destroyed some railings and nearly killed a sentry. King George VI and Queen Elizabeth continued to live in the Palace during the war.

Prince Charles, when he was a bachelor, lived in a three-roomed apartment, plus bathroom, on the second floor of the Palace, its tall windows overlooking The Mall and St James's Park. It was originally decorated by David Hicks and consisted of a study, its walls sombrely painted brown, with a large desk at its centre, bookcases on two walls and a sizeable display cabinet containing a host of precious articles and ornaments in gold, silver and glass, most having been bought by the Prince and not presented as gifts. A sofa and three chairs in front of the desk formed a comfortable conversation area. A connecting door by the long windows led to a sitting-room, decorated in blue and beset with objects and ornaments, acquired mainly on royal tours and visits abroad. Books abounded; in the centre were a sofa and chairs around a glass-topped coffee-table; in a corner stood a large television set, a stereo record-player and video-cassette recorder. His video library includes cassettes of almost all the television programmes in which he has appeared. His bedroom, also in blue, was dominated by a large four-poster bed; the bathroom beyond was adorned with framed original cartoons portraying his family and himself.

Windsor Castle

The favourite residence of reigning monarchs for centuries, Windsor Castle, on a chalk hill south of

Windsor Castle, as depicted in the eighteenth century by J.C. Stadler

the River Thames, occupies nearly 13 acres and is the largest castle in England. Established by William the Conqueror *circa* 1078 as a motte and bailey fortress, surrounded by palisades, it was fortified in stone and enlarged in the twelfth and thirteenth centuries, mainly by Henry III (1216–72). Edward III (1327–77), who founded St George's Chapel and the Order of the Garter in 1348, rebuilt the royal apartments in the Upper Ward. The present chapel dates from 1475. Further improvements and additions were made by Charles II, and slow but considerable reconstruction took place in the reigns of George III, George IV and Queen Victoria: the height of the Round Tower was much increased and other towers were heightened, embellished and crenellated in the Gothic style by Sir Jeffrey Wyatville. Both King George V and King George VI are buried here. Prince Charles has a private apartment in the Castle.

Balmoral Castle

The Castle stands near the River Dee in the heart of the Highlands and the Grampian mountains, south-east of the central massif of the Cairngorms and 49 miles west of Aberdeen. Originally bought on a lease in 1848, the freehold of the Castle and the estate (17,400 acres) was purchased by Prince Albert, husband of Queen Victoria, from the Trustees of the Earl of Fife in 1852, their intention being to use the Castle as a holiday retreat. The whitewashed granite building was redesigned, enlarged and rebuilt on his instructions. 'My dearest Albert's own creation', wrote Queen Victoria, who laid the foundation stone of the new Castle on 28 September 1853. Prince Albert also designed the new layout of the gardens. Planted with conifers and other trees, several quite rare, the gardens are now open to the public – as are Queen Victoria's garden cottage and the sunken garden made for Queen Mary.

Prince Albert and Queen Victoria first ventured to Scotland for health reasons and were both much taken by the country and its people. 'Scotland has made a most favourable impression on us both,' she wrote, after their first visit in 1842. 'The country is full of beauty, of a severe and grand character, perfect for sport of all kinds, and the air remarkably pure and light in comparison with what we have here.'

The Royal Family today spend part of their summer holiday at Balmoral every year.

The Palace of Holyrood House in Edinburgh also becomes a temporary home for the Royal Family on their annual visit to the Scottish capital.

Craigowan and Delnadamph

The Prince and Princess of Wales will spend part of every summer holiday in Scotland on the Balmoral estate, either at nearby Birkhall, the Queen Mother's Deeside home, at Craigowan, or in Balmoral Castle. Either Birkhall or Craigowan could in time become their permanent Scottish home.

Craigowan, a ten-minute walk away from Balmoral Castle and situated near the Castle's nine-hole golf-course, has in recent years been particularly favoured as a 'holiday' home by the Royal Family, who prefer, with comfort and economy in mind, not to live in regal splendour on their great estates. The house, which usually accommodates senior members of the Queen's Household, has become popular with

Overleaf: Balmoral Castle in Aberdeenshire, Grampian, where the Royal Family spend part of every summer

Prince Philip and his eldest son, who stay there when visiting Balmoral on weekend shoots.

Last year, the Queen bought Delnadamph Lodge for a reputed £200,000. It is a solid two-storey Victorian ten-bedroomed lodge, situated on a 6,700-acre estate near the source of the River Don and a ten-mile hike across the Grampian mountains north of Balmoral. The estate itself, which the Queen bought five years ago for an estimated £750,000, is largely treeless, bleak and barren, but possesses some of the best grouse moors in the Highlands. It was rumoured earlier this year that Delnadamph would be the Queen's wedding gift to the Prince and Princess of Wales. But the house would need extensive modernization before it could become a home: there is no central-heating and the kitchen's cooker is fuelled by Calor Gas.

Sandringham and Osborne

Sandringham House, in Norfolk, is a few miles east of The Wash, and eight miles north of King's Lynn. The original house and the 7,000-acre estate were bought in 1862 by Queen Victoria for her eldest son, Albert Edward, the stocky twenty-year-old Prince of Wales – six months after the death of his father, Prince Albert. The Queen had come to an arrangement about the house with the Prime Minister, Lord Palmerston, whose stepson, a middle-aged widower (some said he was Palmerston's illegitimate son) was only too pleased to receive £220,000 for the estate and all thereon, as it had cost him just £76,000 twenty-six years before.

The young Prince of Wales' ideas about the house altered radically after his engagement in September 1862 to Princess Alexandra of Denmark, and in the months before their wedding (in March 1863) he was often at Sandringham, fretting over the renovations and harrying designers, builders and surveyors. The Princess of Wales first stayed in the newly painted and plastered house that Easter, and was delighted with it. Although the house was a pleasant abode in the summer, it suffered from damp during the winter, and after the Christmas holidays, Princess Alexandra returned to Marlborough House, the young couple's London residence, suffering severely from rheumatism. This affliction, which made her lame for life, was blamed by her doctors on Sandringham, and the Prince of Wales resolved that the house would have to be completely rebuilt. The reconstruction and the building of a new wing began in 1869 and was finished in November 1870; the first house-warming was a glittering county ball for 300 guests on 9 December.

The Prince and Princess of Wales at home in the saloon at Sandringham House in 1880. Queen Victoria arranged for her son, 'Bertie', to buy the house in 1862.

Twenty-one years later, on 31 October 1891, a fire at Sandringham heralded a series of events that would change the succession. The Prince of Wales and his family were not in residence at the time of the fire but, undaunted, assembled in the house on 9 November for the Prince's fiftieth birthday, by which time most of the damage had been repaired. The following day, the Prince's second son, Prince George, fell ill with typhoid and was moved to Marlborough House. He was said to be out of danger on 7 December, the day that his elder brother, Eddy, Duke of Clarence, then aged twenty-seven, announced his engagement to Princess Mary of Teck. They were to be married three months later. The family were together again at Sandringham for Christmas and the New Year. It was bitterly cold and foggy: there was ice-hockey and skating on the lakes, and the shooting parties that went out froze. On the Duke of Clarence's twenty-eighth birthday, 8 January 1892, he came downstairs to inspect his presents and to be congratulated, but soon retired to bed with influenza. Pneumonia developed, and the following week he was delirious. Early on 14 January the Duke died.

Prince George, now created Duke of York, married his brother's former *fiancée*, Princess Mary, in July 1893, honeymooning at York Cottage on the estate – 'which I regret and think rather *unlucky* and sad', wrote Queen Victoria.

King George V and King George VI both died at Sandringham; the former in January 1936 and the latter in February 1952. The Royal Family spend every Christmas at Sandringham, and of all the royal residences it is the one that is most like a home.

In 1967, a temporary home was provided for Prince Charles on the Sandringham estate when he was studying at Cambridge. This was Wood Farm, a commodious grey-stone cottage, once the home of the Queen's local physician, Dr Ansell. It was renovated and redecorated for his use at weekends. When Sandringham itself was given an overhaul in 1975–6, at a cost of about £250,000, the Royal Family lodged at Wood Farm. It is still used as a guest-house and is a favoured secondary residence of the Queen.

The Sandringham estate now covers over 20,000 acres and includes six villages within a five-mile radius of the house. On the estate 3,200 acres are farmed by the Queen; 12,000 are let to tenant farmers; 1,780 are given over to the Sandringham Country Park; 470 to parkland; 430 to small-holders; and 243 acres to the royal stud. The estate has proved to be a successful business venture, unlike Balmoral, which is run at a loss.

As at Balmoral, Windsor Castle, and the Queen's Gallery and the Royal Mews in Buckingham Palace, the house and grounds at Sandringham are open for part of the year to the public – in the case of Sandringham, from April to September.

Osborne House, on the Isle of Wight near East Cowes, was designed by Prince Albert, assisted by Thomas Cubitt, and completed by the latter in 1846. The original Osborne House and estate of 1,000 acres were bought for £26,000 from Lady Blatchford. However, the new house, built around cast-iron girders, lavishly furnished and decorated to Prince Albert's orders and with various modern improvements such as electricity, cost about £200,000.

The house was presented to the nation in 1902 by Edward VII and is not strictly speaking a royal residence today but remains as a memorial to Queen Victoria whose state apartments are open to the public. She described Osborne as 'a perfect little Paradise' and wrote: 'We can walk about anywhere by ourselves without fear of being followed and mobbed . . . It is impossible to imagine a prettier spot – valleys and woods which would be beautiful anywhere; but all this near the sea . . . is quite perfection.' Queen Victoria died in her bedroom at Osborne on the evening of Tuesday, 22 January 1901. She was eighty-one, and had reigned for over sixty-three years.

Opposite above: Prince George, Duke of York, married Princess Mary of Teck on 6 July 1893. They honeymooned at York Cottage on the Sandringham estate.

Opposite below: Osborne House was designed by Prince Albert. Part of it is now a convalescent home.

CHAPTER 8

The Princes of Wales

Prince Charles is the twenty-first Prince of Wales, the first being Edward of Caernarvon, later Edward II (1284–1327), the son of Edward I (1272–1307). Before the title was misappropriated by Edward I, it belonged to the Welsh, being used in the late ninth century as a generic term for the six sons of Rhodri Mawr, a warrior lord who united the Welsh in the same period that King Alfred united the Christian English against the pagan Danes.

Edward I consolidated his conquest of north Wales by building a series of great castles, and in 1284, in the workers' camp surrounding the fortress that was under construction at Caernarvon, his wife, Queen Eleanor, gave birth to a son, Edward. King Edward was forty-five; two other sons had already died, and four months after the birth of Edward, the heir apparent, Alfonso, aged ten, also died. The christening of the future Edward II at Caernarvon was lavishly staged. But the legend of the King presenting his naked, new-born son to the Welsh lords, saying 'Your man!' ('*Eich Dyn!*'), is probably an Elizabethan invention. Sixteen years later, young Edward was invested as *the first British Prince of Wales* and Earl of Chester at Lincoln. This was in February 1301, during a winter break in his bellicose father's campaigns against the Scots.

Just over half of the twenty-one princes of Wales – twelve – eventually became King. *The second Prince of Wales*, Edward of Woodstock, eldest son of Edward III, was not one of them. Distinguished after his death by the nickname the 'Black Prince', he is also notable as the first English Duke to be ennobled in England as the Duke of Cornwall. Previously Cornwall had been an earldom, usually held by a brother of the King. Edward of Woodstock was twelve when he was invested as Prince of Wales, and sixteen when in 1346 he fought at the Battle of Crécy. Among those he killed was the old and blind King of Bohemia, whose crest was an eagle's wing and whose motto was *Ich Dien* (I Serve). Legend says that Edward took the old King's motto as well as his life and for some reason altered the eagle's wing into a set of ostrich feathers.

The Black Prince was said to have been the most eligible bachelor in Europe, tall, handsome and brave, 'the flower of chivalry'; he spent most of his time in sporting and military pursuits with like-minded companions. His father expected him to make a politically advantageous marriage and wed Marguerite, only child of the Count of Flanders and the young widow and heiress of the Duke of Burgundy.

Left: HRH The Prince of Wales, 1 July 1969

Right: Edward I (1239–1307) presenting the future first British Prince of Wales to the Welsh Lords in 1284.

Left: Edward of Woodstock (1330–76), the second Prince of Wales, became known as the 'Black Prince'.

Above: Prince Arthur (1486–1502), the eighth Prince of Wales, and elder brother of Henry VIII

Disliking such an arranged match, the Black Prince eventually chose his cousin, the Countess of Kent, another wealthy widow – she was two years older than him – and reputed to be *la plus belle de tout le royaume d'Angleterre et la plus amoureuse*. It was not a suitable match, but a love match all the same. For the Prince had known her all his life – she was brought up in the Queen's household – and despite mounting paternal and political pressure on him to marry and secure male heirs, he had waited, it seems, until she was widowed and free to marry him. When her husband, Sir Thomas Holland, died in 1360 – the Fair Maid of Kent was a Countess in her own right – the Prince of Wales obtained the necessary licence and a dispensation from the Pope, then at Avignon.

The marriage contract of Edward, Prince of Wales and Joan, Countess of Kent, was signed at the Archbishop's Palace at Lambeth in October 1361. The wedding ceremony was performed four days after the contract was signed, on Sunday, 10 October, in the newly built Garter Chapel of St George in Windsor. No contemporary descriptions of the ceremony have survived, but the new Princess of Wales' gown must have been gorgeous, for it was said of her that 'her love of dress was notorious in an age of extreme luxury and show. She affected the most costly robes of irridescent shot silk. Her wardrobe was overcrowded with hundreds of dresses . . . wonderfully jewelled belts, costly furs, silks from Lyons, Aleppo and Alexandria . . . Her lofty coifs were radiant and her person glittered with jewels.' In commemoration of the marriage the Prince dedicated a chapel; the Princess commissioned a bed 'of red velvet, decorated with ostrich feathers in silver, leopards' heads in gold.' She bore him two sons: Edmund, who predeceased him, and Richard, who became *the third Prince of Wales* and later succeeded his grandfather as Richard II.

The fourth Prince of Wales, Henry of Monmouth, was the second (and last) to be born in Wales, in 1387, and through the belligerence of his father, Henry of Bolingbroke (later Henry IV) became Henry V.

Henry VII begat two Princes of Wales, Arthur of Winchester, invested in 1489 when he was three, and Henry of Greenwich (Henry VIII). Prince Arthur, *the eighth Prince of Wales*, physically frail, was probably educated to death, his father having decided that his eldest son should be the perfect Renaissance prince, a *non-pareil* in scholastic and physical achievements. Negotiations for his marriage to the youngest daughter of the King of Spain were begun while both he and Princess Catherine of Aragon were in their infancy. Naked, he was inspected by the Spanish ambassadors before they reported back to their King. Henry VII demanded a dowry of 200,000 crowns, a fortune, and that Catherine be taught to drink wine – 'for the water in England is not drinkable'. They were married three times by proxy before Catherine, aged sixteen, set sail for England in May 1501, reaching Plymouth after a four-month nightmare journey bedevilled by adverse winds and high seas. Her entourage advanced towards London so slowly that King Henry, becoming impatient, took the Prince of Wales to meet her – a move that upset the Spaniards' feelings of propriety. Henry VII said he 'might look on her if he liked'. Leaving the fifteen-year-old Prince Arthur in the pouring rain outside Dogmersfield in Hampshire, the King went on ahead into the town only to find that the young Princess had gone to bed. Henry insisted on seeing her, saying that even if 'she were in bed he meant to see and speak to her; for that was his mind and the whole intent of his coming.' Eventually the little Princess received him. The Prince of Wales arrived within half an hour and was introduced to his future bride by the King. The couple – Catherine, at sixteen, was ten months older than the Prince – then plighted their troth in person, and the King and his son withdrew.

On 13 November Princess Catherine made a triumphal entry into London. Church bells rang, choirs sang hymns of welcome, and the people cheered. She was met at St George's-in-the-Fields by the King's second son, Henry, Duke of York, then aged ten, a hulking boy on horseback, dressed in velvet and with amber hair and rosy cheeks. He escorted her into London: she sitting in a richly caparisoned chair perched on a mule – a Spanish custom. A contemporary observed that 'her hair was auburn and it spilled to her shoulders. Her hat, shaped like that of a cardinal, was tied with lace of

Catherine of Aragon (1486–1536) married Prince Arthur, in 1501. He died in 1502 and she became Henry VIII's first queen after his accession in 1509. Painting by Michael Sittow

gold and a coif of rich carnation colour held it to her head.' The following morning, Sunday, Prince Henry, now dressed in white satin trimmed with gold, called for her at dawn – tradition demanded Prince Arthur and Catherine should be married before 10 o'clock. The wedding took place in St Paul's Cathedral, the first time St Paul's and the City of London had witnessed such an event. It was an extravagant, theatrical affair. Inside the cathedral the walkway ended in a circular dais, large enough for eight persons, and the whole structure was covered with a fine worsted red cloth. To the north of the dais sat the King and Queen Elizabeth, with members of their family, in a latticed box. The Count de Cabra, standing proxy for King Ferdinand, led Princess Catherine along the walkway onto the dais, where the Prince of Wales, dressed in white satin like

Henry VIII became the ninth Prince of Wales when Prince Arthur died in 1502. He was Prince of Wales until 1509 when he became King. Painting by an unknown artist, c. 1520

his younger brother, and the Archbishop of Canterbury, were waiting. The bride's wedding-dress attracted much comment, combining such features as a voluminous mantilla and an early crinoline. She wore 'upon her head a coif of white silk, with a scarf bordered with gold and pearl and precious stones, five inches and a half broad, which veiled a great part of her visage and person. Her gown was very large, both the sleeves and also the body, with many plaits; and beneath the waist, certain round hoops, bearing out the gown from her body after the manner of her country.'

After the service, mass was said and the Prince endowed the new Princess of Wales with a third of his property. As the royal couple left the cathedral, bells rang out in the City and once again the populace cheered as the wedding-party rode to the Bishop of Bath's palace for their nuptial dinner – 'a sumptuous feast and plentiful dancings and disguisings.' It lasted all day. At night, Prince Arthur and his bride were ceremoniously led to and ensconced in the marriage bed. The following morning the Prince, it is said, merrily called for a drink, 'which heretofore times he was not accustomed to do. One of his chamberlains, marvelling, asked him the cause of his drought, at which the prince answered merrily: "I have this night been in the midst of Spain, which is a hot region . . ."' It was a royal joke, in more ways than one. The marriage of the student prince was probably never consummated. Prince Arthur fell sick, some said of the plague, and on 2 April 1502, less than five months after the wedding, he died.

His young widow, the Princess of Wales, eight years later became the first wife of *the ninth Prince of Wales*, that 'hulking boy' who had brought her to St Paul's and was now Henry VIII.

Curiously, Henry VIII never bestowed the title of Prince of Wales on his only son, Edward, who became King in 1547 when he was ten. James I revived the title of Prince of Wales, investing his eldest son, Henry of Stirling, as *the tenth* in 1610, when he was sixteen. Prince Henry was apparently a paragon among princes: his fine features and physique matched by his intellect, learning and athletic skills. As with that previous prince of great potential, Arthur, he could speak and write Latin, Greek, French and Spanish, was skilled in music and the arts, archery and jousting, and a capable theologian and historian. King James, in whom justice, clemency, magnanimity, liberality, constancy and humility were as shaky as his morality and kingly capabilities, wrote a manual for his eldest son acclaiming these qualities as princely virtues. Yet most if not all the precepts in his book, *Basilikon Doron* (Gift of the King), would doubtless meet with the approval of the parents of any Prince of Wales.

He wrote: 'Keep God sparingly in your mouth, but abundantly in your heart . . . The whole Scripture consisteth of two things, a command and a prohibition: to do such things and to abstain from the contrary. Obey in both; nor think it enough to abstain from evil and do no good.' Of the Prince's parents: 'I grant ye we have our faults which . . . should serve ye for examples to meditate upon and mend in your own person, but should not be a matter of discourse to others.' On marriage: 'Consider that marriage is the greatest earthly felicity or misery that can come to a man. Keep your body clean and unpolluted and so give it to your wife, to whom only it belongeth . . . For how can ye justly crave to be joined to a good and pure virgin if your body be polluted? . . . Why should one be clean and the other defiled? . . . Choose you a wife as I advise you to choose your servants, that she be of a whole clean race, not subjected to hereditary sickness of the soul or body;

Henry, Prince of Wales, with the Earl of Essex, in the Hunting Field, by an unknown artist. Henry Frederick (1594–1612), eldest son of James I of England, was tenth Prince of Wales.

for if a man be careful to breed horses and dogs of good kinds, how much more careful should he be for the breed of his own loins?'

But as with Prince Arthur, of whom so much was also expected, Prince Henry died, aged nineteen, before he was able to put into practice what his father had preached, and again it was the second son who became *the eleventh Prince of Wales* and succeeded to the throne as Charles I.

The eldest son of Charles I became *the twelfth Prince of Wales* soon after his birth in 1630. But his father's attitude to parliament, politics and God not only marred his formal education but made this heir apparent appear like one most unlikely to succeed. Yet the Civil War and his years in exile taught young Prince Charles more about kingship than a library of books, and as Charles II he became one of the most capable, if self-indulgent, of kings. But despite his baker's dozen of acknowledged royal bastards, no children were produced by his Queen.

His brother, James II, likewise failed to produce a legitimate male heir, one acceptable to a Protestant Parliament, and *the thirteenth Prince of Wales*, James Francis Edward (the Old Pretender) was thrice unlucky in 1688 when the rampant Whigs deprived him when he was only six months old of his titles, his country and his hereditary rights.

In 1714 a middle-aged German prince, George Louis, the Elector of Hanover, who hardly spoke any English, became king in succession to the childless Queen Anne. The new King took his time leaving the pleasures of Hanover. He brought with him his daughter-in-law, Caroline of Ansbach, and his only son, George Augustus (1683–1760), who became *the fourteenth Prince of Wales* in November 1714.

The new Prince and Princess of Wales, at the direction of the King, left their seven-year-old son, Frederick Louis, in Hanover when they came to England. There this 'florid, mild-faced kind of boy' was brought up harshly by his tutors. They reported his unruly behaviour to his disinterested parents and deplored his ability 'to drink as deep as any German baron'. Lady Mary Wortley Montague, on the other hand, said of the boy in 1716: 'He is the most agreeable young man it is possible to imagine, without being the least handsome. His person is little but well made and genteel. He has a liveliness in his eyes which is indescribable, and the most obliging address that can be conceived.'

Prince Charles dancing with his sister, Mary, at a ball at The Hague during his exile. Prince Charles (1630–85), later Charles II, was the eleventh Prince of Wales. Painting by Janssens

At the time of the accession of George II in 1728, Prince Frederick, according to Thomas Carlyle, 'was eager to be wedded to Wilhelmina (the Princess Royal of Prussia) as one grand, and at present grandest source of his existence.' The marriage was virtually sanctioned by George I, but he died before the contract was signed; and such was the antipathy between George II and Frederick William of Prussia that the match became unthinkable.

Prince Frederick came to England in December 1728, when he was twenty-one. It was a cheerless arrival. The *Daily Post* said: 'His Royal Highness Prince Frederick came to Whitechapel about seven

in the evening and proceeded thence privately in a hackney coach to St James . . . and was thence conducted to Her Majesty's apartment.' He was received with a cold embrace from Queen Caroline and two casual fingers of his father's hand.

Soon after his arrival, Frederick was created Prince of Wales, *the fifteenth*, in January 1729. But the title and its accompanying revenues did little to improve the Prince's lot. He saw marriage as the only means of escape from his parents, who for some reason, never properly explained, loathed him. 'Fritz's popularity makes me vomit!' said his mother. She called him an 'avaricious, sordid monster' and said he would sell his Crown to the Pretender for half a million pounds. She exclaimed: 'My dear first-born is the greatest ass and the greatest liar and the greatest *canaille* and the greatest beast in the whole world, and I heartily wish he were out of it!'

Realizing the Prince's predicament, the Dowager Duchess of Marlborough shrewdly offered him

£100,000, in the form of a dowry for her favourite grand-daughter, Lady Diana Spencer. Frederick readily agreed to accept both, and the wedding was arranged. However, the plot was rumbled by Walpole's spies and the marriage never took place.

The King then proposed that his son should marry the Danish Princess Royal. But the Prince of Wales rejected her, saying she was deformed and an imbecile, and that the idea was just a bad joke on the part of his father. In the end, as Frederick's financial position became more desperate, he agreed to marry Princess Augusta of Saxe-Gotha. As a result, he had to dispose of his mistresses, who included Anne Vane, formerly the mistress of Lord Hervey, the Queen's Vice-Chamberlain.

Princess Augusta arrived at Greenwich on 25 April 1736. The Prince, aged twenty-nine, hurried to meet the shy, rather gawky girl of seventeen who spoke no English at all. He took her for a trip up-river, showing her off in his royal barge, in which she sat silently, clutching a rag doll. The following day they set off for London but were an hour late in arriving at the Palace. The King was in a rage; but the Princess soon reduced his wrath, according to Lord Hervey, for 'as soon as she came, she threw herself all along the floor, first at the King's and then at the Queen's feet, who both took her up and embraced her.'

Hervey said she was 'rather tall, and had health and youth enough in her face, joined to a very modest and good-natured look, to make her countenance not disagreeable. But her person, from being very ill-made . . . her long arms and her motions awkward, had, in spite of all the finery of jewels and brocade, an ordinary air which no trappings could cover or exalt.' The Earl of Egmont, who noted that her face 'was much pitted with smallpox and had a great colour from the heat of the day,' concluded more kindly: 'She has a peculiar affability of behaviour and a very sweetness of countenance, mixed with innocence, cheerfulness and sense.'

The wedding took place shortly before 9 o'clock that night in the Chapel Royal in St James's Palace. The Earl of Egmont wrote in his diary: 'There was a prodigious crowd, for the King's pleasure was that there should be no procession, but lords, gentlemen and ladies might fill the chapel as they came, without order or distinction.' Everyone was gorgeously attired. The Princess wore 'a robe of crimson velvet, turned back with several rows of ermine' and on her head 'a crown with one bar as Princess of Wales'. The Queen wore a yellow silk robe and jewels 'of immense value'. The King was magnificently garbed in gold brocade embroidered with larger silver flowers and diamonds. The 2nd Duke of Marlborough reputedly paid £400 for his splendid coat of white velvet and gold. The chapel itself, according to Egmont 'was adorned with tapestry, velvet and gold lace, all the pews taken down, and benches raised one above another for the convenience and to make room for spectators. Over the altar was placed the organ, and a gallery made for the musicians. An anthem composed by Handel for the occasion was wretchedly sung by Abbot, Gates, Lee, Bird and a boy. The King gave the Princess in marriage, and during the ceremony the Queen was obliged to explain to the Princess in the French or German tongue the marriage oath.'

The Music Party, by Philippe Mercier, c. 1733. Prince Frederick, fifteenth Prince of Wales (1707–51), son of George II, with his three eldest sisters, playing in the Banqueting House, Hampton Court

Lord Hervey, never slow to belittle the Prince of Wales, wrote: 'At supper nothing remarkable happened but the Prince's eating several glasses of jelly, and every time he took one turning about, laughing, and winking on some of his servants. The King went after supper to the Prince's apartment whilst the Queen undressed the Princess, and when they were in bed everybody passed through their bedchamber to see them, where there was nothing remarkable but the Prince's nightcap, which was some inches higher than any grenadier's cap in the whole army. There were various reports on what did and did not pass this night after the company retired. The Queen and Lord Hervey agreed that the bride looked extremely tired with the fatigues of the day, and so well refreshed next morning, that they concluded she had slept very sound.'

The Prince's life with his wife was quite happy. He was a good husband and also a good father, according to a contemporary, who wrote: 'He loved to have his children with him, always appeared most happy when in the bosom of his family, left them with regret and met them again with smiles, kisses and tears.'

Prince Frederick, an amiable patron of the arts, liked to dabble in them himself, writing poems and music, a play and a book; he played the 'cello and acted. He also rode, fished, shot and played cricket – he was captain of Surrey. He never, however, succeeded his father. He was killed by a cricket-ball, struck in a game with his children. It hit an abscess, which burst and he died, aged forty-three, of blood poisoning. On hearing the sad news of his death, the King, who was playing cards, merely remarked to his mistress: *'Fritz ist todt'*, and went on playing.

The quarrelling over the education of Prince Frederick's eldest son, the turmoil of tutors coming and going, left *the sixteenth Prince of Wales*, George William Frederick (later George III) less educated than most of his predecessors. Lord Waldegrave said that his tutors, although men of learning, 'had but little weight and influence. The mother and the nursery always prevailed.' His father in his will

Left: Prince George William Frederick, (1738–1820), sixteenth Prince of Wales and later George III. Painting by Jean-Etienne Liotard (1702–89)

Right: Prince George (1762–1830), seventeenth Prince of Wales, aged twenty-nine later Prince Regent and George IV. Painting by George Stubbs, 1791

instructed young George, who became the sixteenth Prince of Wales in 1751 aged thirteen, to be 'Just, Humane, Generous and Brave, to live with economy', and 'convince the Nation that You are not only an Englishman born and bred, but . . . by inclination.'

Prince George was a slow and honest, pious and oddly innocent boy, with a serious view of his position and indeed of life. When his teenage brother, Edward, said one day: 'Brother, when you and I are grown, you shall be married, but I will keep a mistress', George retorted: 'Be quiet, Eddy . . . There must be no mistresses at all.'

He was twenty-two when he succeeded his grandfather as George III, and as he was already King when he married Princess Charlotte of Mecklenburg-Strelitz, she became Queen and was never a Princess of Wales. Their first child, George Augustus Frederick, was born on 12 August 1762 and was created Prince of Wales five days later. He was *the seventeenth Prince of Wales.*

He had to wait nearly sixty years before ascending the throne as George IV, although during the last nine years of his father's life he ruled as Prince Regent. His education was extremely strict and severe and errors were disciplined, sometimes with a flogging. He and his brothers (George III had fifteen children) studied for seven hours every day. Their meal-breaks were described in a contemporary newspaper: 'The royal children by His Majesty's command get up early, have bread and milk for breakfast and dine on broth and salads . . . They drink no liquor other than whey or milk or water and are sometimes indulged with a glass of weak negus. Supper is the same as breakfast.' This regime, aimed at turning the royal boys into gentlemen-scholars, failed to teach them to be princes or to rule.

Prince George, or Prinny as he became known, revolting against such dullness and discipline, became anything but dull or disciplined. He told his father, who got up at 5 a.m. and used to complain about his eldest son's indolence: 'I find, Sir, however late I rise, that the day is long enough for doing nothing' – a sentiment with which Edward VII when Prince of Wales would have heartily concurred. Prince George accordingly filled his days with as many pleasurable diversions that could be devised. In an age of extreme show and style he led a life of unparalleled extravagance. A leader of fashion, he was spending £10,000 a year on clothes alone by the time he was twenty-one. The cost of his mistresses, card-parties, select suppers and weekly levees at Carlton House, as well as his prodigious gambling

Princess Caroline returned to England in 1820 to claim her rights as queen when the Regent became George IV. She was, however, unsuccessful and died in 1821. A contemporary cartoon

debts, added up to £160,000 by the time he was twenty-three. Like his grandfather, Frederick, he finally resorted to marriage as a means of paying off his debts, although he had vowed: 'I will never marry. My resolution is taken on that subject.' When his debts exceeded half a million pounds, his resolve gave way – despite the fact that he was already married (as he believed) 'in the eyes of God' to one of his many mistresses, Mrs Fitzherbert. A diplomat, the 1st Earl of Malmesbury, was asked to find a bride and fix the contract. King George III, when consulted, chose his niece, Princess Caroline of Brunswick, and Lord Malmesbury was sent to Brunswick in 1794 to conclude the marriage arrangements and instruct the twenty-six-year-old Princess in the ways of the English court.

He found this a difficult task – as he informed his diary: 'If she can get the better of a gossiping habit, she will do very well . . . I make it the daily object of my conversation to urge upon her never to *stoop* to *private* concerns . . . to avoid remarks, and not care what passes in society . . . I also took frequent opportunities of speaking very *seriously* to the Princess Caroline on her not showing due respect to the Duchess her mother, of her sneering and slighting her; and on this point I went perhaps beyond the bounds of *decorum* . . . She *at first* took it amiss, but very soon after admitted the truth of what I said and observed.'

Malmesbury, Princess Caroline and her mother (George III's sister, Princess Augusta) set out from Brunswick at the end of December 1794, but did not arrive in England until the beginning of April, due to the unwelcome attentions of the French and Dutch fleets and fog in the Channel. The Princess was met at Greenwich by Lady Jersey, one of her future husband's mistresses. They travelled by coach from Greenwich to London where, according to Malmesbury 'there was very little crowd and still less applause on the road.'

The first meeting of the sixteen-stone, thirty-two-year-old Prince of Wales and Princess Caroline was faithfully recorded by Malmesbury: 'I, according to the established etiquette, introduced (no one else being in the room) the Princess Caroline to him. She very properly . . . attempted to kneel to him. He raised her (gracefully enough), and embraced her, said barely one word, turned round, retired to a distant part of the apartment, and calling me to him said: "Harris, I am not well; pray get me a glass of brandy." . . . The Princess, left during this short moment alone, was in a state of astonishment . . . I said his Royal Highness was naturally a good deal affected and flurried at this first interview, but she would certainly find him different at dinner.'

But at dinner, *her* behaviour distressed Malmesbury more than that of the Prince: 'It was flippant, rattling, affected railery and wit, and throwing out coarse vulgar hints about Lady Jersey who was present . . . the Prince was evidently disgusted, and this unfortunate dinner fixed his dislike, which . . . the Princess had not the talent to remove; but . . . increased it till it became positive hatred.'

They were married in April 1795 in the Chapel Royal in St James's Palace. A guest observed: 'He looked like death and full of confusion, as if he wished to hide himself from the looks of the whole world.' Malmesbury described the scene thus: 'The ceremony was performed by the Archbishop of Canterbury. The usual etiquette observed – we had assembled in the Queen's apartment; from thence to the usual drawing rooms (very dark). The procession, preceded by the heralds and great officers of the Court (amongst which I was ordered to attend) – walked to the chapel – very crowded – Prince of Wales gave his hat, with a rich diamond button and loop, to Lord Harcourt to hold, and made him a present of it. After the marriage we returned to the Queen's apartment . . . The Prince very civil and gracious, but . . . I could perceive he was not quite sincere, and certainly unhappy; and, as a proof of it, he had manifestly had recourse to wine or spirits.'

The disastrous honeymoon began with a few days at Windsor and then the couple moved to Kempshot House, near Basingstoke, where they were joined by some of the Prince's men friends, who disgusted Caroline by 'sleeping and snoring with their boots on the sofa' and drinking to excess.

They were formally separated soon after their only child, Princess Charlotte, was born, in January 1796. Charlotte later married Prince Leopold of Saxe-Coburg, but died in childbirth. Prinny finally came to the throne in 1820 and ruled for ten years.

Queen Victoria came to the throne in 1837 and married her cousin, 'her beloved Albert' on 10 February 1840. She passed a note to him that morning: 'Dearest, how are you today and have you slept well? I have rested very well, and feel very comfortable today. What weather! I believe, however, the rain will cease. Send one word when you, my most dearly beloved Bridegroom, will be ready. Thy ever-faithful Victoria R.'

Their first son, Prince Albert Edward, was born towards the end of the following year. He was created Prince of Wales, *the eighteenth*, when he was barely a month old.

His education, along with that of his nine brothers and sisters, was carefully and strictly supervised by his father, whose last two directives before he died (in 1861) were that the Prince should visit the Holy Land, which he did, and marry Princess Alexandra of Denmark. A meeting between them was duly arranged.

The Queen, travelling under the name 'La Comtesse de Balmoral', visited her uncle, King Leopold of the Belgians, at his palace at Laeken, near Brussels, in September 1862. The twenty-year-old Prince of Wales went with her. Princess Alexandra, who was only seventeen, was warned to dress simply and not to smile, as the Queen, still in mourning, could not bear to see anyone looking happy. She met with the Queen's approval, although the Queen was moved to tears. She turned to her Wally (Walburga, Lady Paget) and said: 'You, dear Wally, will quite understand what I feel at this moment. You have a husband you love, and you know what I have lost.' The dutiful Prince of Wales told Wally: 'I will take a walk with the Princess Alix in the garden and in three quarters of an hour I will take her into the Grotto, and there I will propose, and I hope it will be to everyone's satisfaction.' Fortunately, it was.

The engagement was announced on 16 September and the wedding fixed for 10 March 1863. In the intervening months Princess Alexandra was obliged to stay with the Queen at Osborne and at Windsor and hear what was expected of her as Princess of Wales and about Prince Albert. She behaved beautifully, concealing her resentment that her father had to stay in a hotel and that her mother had not been invited to England. Queen Victoria was enthusiastic: 'How Albert would have loved her . . . she is so good, so simple, unaffected, frank, bright and cheerful, yet so quiet and gentle . . . she is one of those sweet creatures who seem to come from the skies to help and bless poor mortals and lighten for a time their path.'

The Queen's decision to have the wedding at Windsor and not in London was much criticized, most acidly by *Punch*, who pictured the venue as 'an obscure Berkshire village noted only for an old castle with no sanitary arrangements.'

The day before the wedding the mourning Queen took her son and his *fiancée* to the mausoleum at Frogmore where Prince Albert was buried. She told her diary: 'I opened the shrine and took them in . . . I said: "*He* gives you his blessing!" and joined Alix's

Overleaf: Prince Albert Edward, eldest son of Queen Victoria, married Princess Alexandra of Denmark at St George's Chapel, Windsor Castle, on 10 March 1863. Painting by W.P. Frith

Spy

and Bertie's hands, taking them both in my arms. It was a very touching moment and we all felt it.' There was a rumour that the Queen wanted St George's Chapel to be hung with black, which caused the Prince to exclaim: 'Then I'd better bring my bride in a hearse!' However, although the bridegroom's mother wore black, the 900 guests were permitted to wear their brightest and best uniforms or gowns, and the scene in the chapel was magnificent, glowing with pomp and heraldry. Queen Victoria sat in a wooden alcove overlooking the altar, dressed in her widow's weeds, which were only relieved by the blue of her Garter sash and a little miniature of Prince Albert.

Princess Alexandra, who cried a little in the morning when she left her mother, remarked to the Queen's eldest daughter, the Crown Princess of Prussia: 'You may think that I am marrying Bertie for his position; but if he were a cowboy I would love him just the same and marry no one else.' Her gown, of white satin, was decked with garlands of orange blossom, with swathes of white tulle and Honiton lace. As she prepared to enter the Chapel, the eight bridesmaids – 'as ugly girls as you could wish to see,' according to Lady Somerset – placed a lengthy silver train on her shoulders. The bridegroom, his 5ft 7ins raised by built-up heels, wore an Order of the Garter cloak over a general's uniform. The Queen wrote in her diary:

> The trumpets sounded again, and our boy, supported by Ernest C[oburg] and Fritz, all in Garter robes, entered; Bertie looking pale and nervous. He bowed to me, and during the long wait for his bride kept constantly looking up at me, with an anxious, clinging look, which touched me much. At length she appeared, the band playing Handel's 'Processional March', with her eight bridesmaids looking very lovely. She was trembling and very pale. Dearest Albert's 'Chorale' was sung, which affected me much, and then the service proceeded. When it was over, the young couple looked up at me, and I gave them an affectionate nod and kissed my hand to sweet Alix. They left together, immediately followed by *all* the others, Beethoven's 'Hallelujah Chorus' being played.

The wedding breakfast in Windsor Castle was not attended by the Queen, who ate alone. She watched from a castle window, with tears in her eyes, as the happy couple drove off on their honeymoon, which lasted a week and was spent at Osborne House on the Isle of Wight.

The Prince of Wales' standard

The Prince of Wales remained as such for fifty-nine years, while his mother's reign lasted, becoming the longest of any British King or Queen. She died in January 1901. By then, the Prince's eldest son, the Duke of Clarence, had also died, and his second son, Prince George, whose career as a naval officer had been as pleasant to him as it was promising, suddenly became the heir apparent, then Duke of York, and *the nineteenth Prince of Wales*.

King George V's eldest son was also destined never to be crowned as King, although he was Prince of Wales, *the twentieth*, for twenty-five years. As Edward VIII he reigned for less than eleven months. He chose to abdicate in December 1936 and to marry Mrs Simpson. As a result, the line of succession changed direction again, settling on George V's second son, the Duke of York, who became George VI.

Charles, *the twenty-first Prince of Wales* – soldier, sailor, airman, parachutist, diplomat, businessman, ambassador, history graduate, linguist, archaeologist, horseman, skin-diver, fisherman, musician, actor, comedian and writer – is the most versatile, well-informed, popular, academically and athletically successful Prince of Wales of them all.

Left: Prince George, Duke of York, became the nineteenth Prince of Wales in 1901 on the death of Queen Victoria.

CHAPTER 9

The Months before the Engagement

In November 1977, Miss Ruth Rudge, the headmistress of West Heath School allowed Lady Diana to go home for the weekend, a special weekend in that the Prince of Wales had been asked to stay and shoot at Althorp. Lady Diana arrived on the Saturday morning and joined the guns on the last drive before lunch. It was then, in a ploughed field on the Althorp estate that the Prince first noticed her – 'a splendid sixteen-year-old, full of fun' as he described her later. Although their families were well acquainted, and their paths must have crossed before, especially at Sandringham, Prince Charles would never have shown more than a polite interest in a girl twelve years his junior. She was still a schoolgirl when Lady Sarah formally introduced the Prince to her.

Over the next two years, Lady Diana was a not infrequent guest of the Queen at Sandringham and Balmoral. In January 1979 she was in a shooting party at Sandringham that included the Prince of Wales and Prince Andrew. A year later, in February 1980, she stayed with the Queen at Wood Farm on the Sandringham estate in a house-party that included the Prince of Wales and his cousin, Amanda Knatchbull. During the summer of 1980 she was among the guests who were invited to attend various royal parties and outings including a trip to Cowdray Park, near Midhurst, in Sussex. The Prince of Wales was playing polo for *Les Diables Bleus* and Lady Diana, with the rest of the party, watched from Lord Cowdray's stand within the members' enclosure.

But it was not until the first week of August 1980, during Cowes Week, that Lady Diana, now nineteen, became the principal guest of the Prince of Wales on board the Royal Yacht *Britannia*, moored off Cowes on the Isle of Wight. She demonstrated her sense of humour by ducking her host in the Solent when she flipped the mast of his wind-surfer. It was a young party, which included Prince Andrew, Prince Edward and their cousins, James and Marina Ogilvy.

Lady Diana had spent much of that summer, 1980, in Scotland, some of it with her mother and stepfather on the Isle of Seil. Early in September she returned to Balmoral, ostensibly to help look after the new-born baby of her sister, Lady Jane Fellowes. She did not accompany the Royal Family and their guests to the Braemar Games or to church, where press photographers lay in wait. However, one of their number, armed with a telephoto-lens, spotted her watching the Prince of Wales salmon fishing on

Left: Lady Diana Spencer seen leaving her flat on 12 November 1980, when there was much speculation that Prince Charles would announce his engagement to her on his thirty-second birthday.

Right: Prince Charles windsurfing at Cowes in August 1980

Overleaf: In September 1980 Lady Diana was seen watching Prince Charles salmon fishing on the River Dee.

the River Dee. When this photograph was published, her association with the Prince of Wales ceased to be a secret, and the Fleet Street gossip columnists began to buzz and speculate. She was named as 'The New Girl for Charles' and headlines proclaimed 'He's in Love Again' by the time she returned to London.

For the next five months her flat in South Kensington was under siege by photographers and reporters. Using binoculars, some peered into the bedroom windows of her flat from the lecture room of the public library opposite. Every morning, when she left for the kindergarten where she worked, she was photographed, followed and questioned. Annoyed but still amused by all the absurd attention, she refused to be drawn, even into denials, responding to questions with a blush or a smile. However, she told one reporter: 'You know I can't say anything about the Prince or my feelings for him,' and added, 'I'm saying that off my own bat. No one has told me to stay quiet.'

The kindergarten school, Young England, where she worked, was also besieged. She complained that 'all this fuss is disrupting my work with the children.' But to dissipate some of the demands she agreed to be photographed 'because the photographers asked me politely and they had been waiting a long time.' She posed with two of the children in the garden in front of the school. Another photographer, an Italian, bent on getting an exclusive photograph, tried to enter the school through a lavatory window. Yet another, dressed as a road-sweeper, patrolled the pavement outside the school.

Despite the unremitting attentions of the world's press, Lady Diana and the Prince of Wales managed to see each other without it being known. In October, before the Queen Mother returned to England after her holiday at her Deeside home at Birkhall, she was joined by her grandson and Lady Diana. The Prince of Wales' book, *The Old Man of Lochnagar*, written originally for Prince Edward and set in Balmoral, was published later that month; the author gave a copy to Lady Diana.

During October little was seen of the Prince with Lady Diana, and speculation about their friendship began to wane – but not for long. On 24 October the Prince of Wales rode his horse, Allibar, in the Clun Handicap Race for amateur riders – a three-mile steeplechase at Ludlow in Shropshire. It was the Prince's first ride over fences, although the previous March he had ridden a horse called Long Wharf in a flat race at Plumpton, when he finished second. Lady Diana drove to Ludlow to watch him. He rode creditably well and came in second, although he admitted later that 'about half way through the race, my concentration seemed to be distracted – I had to work hard to get it back.' He won £294 with £1,000 going to the winner, Hello Louis, who won by six lengths. Lady Diana backed the Prince each way, making a fair return on his price of 10 to 1. 'It's marvellous,' she said. 'He's worked really hard to get his weight down; he's only three pounds overweight.'

They left Ludlow to stay with the Prince of Wales' friends Lieutenant Colonel and Mrs Andrew Parker-Bowles in their Wiltshire home near Chippenham, and on Saturday the Prince and his host went cubbing with the Beaufort Hunt. On their return, Lady Diana left the house to meet them in the drive, only to vanish inside when she saw the ever-attendant throng of pressmen. During that weekend Prince Charles drove Lady Diana to Tetbury to show her Highgrove House.

The following weekend they returned to the Parker-Bowles' for the opening meet of the Beaufort Hunt. The meet was held at the Hunt Kennels situated in Badminton Park and the Prince of Wales, as was his habit, joined the hunt shortly after they had 'moved off', so that the sightseers who had come to see him would not disrupt the meet. It was a fine day and the Prince and his host had some excellent sport; this time Lady Diana stayed indoors with Camilla Parker-Bowles.

On Tuesday, 4 November 1980, six of Princess Margaret's closest friends gave a dance for her at the Ritz Hotel in celebration of her fiftieth birthday. Lady Diana was among the 200 guests; she was also invited to the dinner given before the dance for members of the Royal Family and their friends. The Prince of Wales sat between Lady Diana and Lady Jane Wellesley.

The next day the Prince of Wales went on an official visit to the West Country and stayed that night on the Royal Train in a siding at Staverton in Wiltshire. Lady Diana, still tired after the dance the night before, stayed in her flat and went to bed early – the night that the *Sunday Mirror* later alleged they had spent together on the train. At the same time a rumour spread that the Prince of Wales was going to announce his engagement to Lady Diana on his thirty-second birthday, Friday, 14 November. It was a suggestion that was strongly denied by her sister, Lady Sarah McCorquodale. Lady Diana slipped out of Coleherne Court and went by train to King's Lynn in Norfolk, from where she travelled to Sandringham in an old Ford Cortina and entered the house unnoticed. The press, lying in wait for her, remained ignorant of her presence for the entire weekend. After her departure, when they discovered she had been a guest for the weekend, their persistent presence provoked the Prince to ask: 'Haven't you got any wives to go to?'

Lady Diana with two of the children at the Young England kindergarten school in Pimlico

During the official tour of India and Nepal in November 1980 Prince Charles undertook a three-day trek in the Himalayas.

The spurious train story appeared in the *Sunday Mirror* on 16 November. The story produced an indignant response from the Queen, and through her press secretary, Michael Shea, she asked for an apology. The newspaper's editor refused to comply with the request, but agreed to print Shea's letter the following Sunday – the same day that the Prince of Wales flew to India and Nepal at the beginning of an official tour. Lady Diana denied the allegations, telling reporters: 'I want to get the record straight. The story was completely false. I was not on the Royal Train when they said and have never been on the Royal Train. I don't even know what it looks like. I stayed in that evening with my flatmates.' Later this story was corroborated by her flatmate, Anne Bolton, who said the report was 'an absolute load of rubbish' and that Lady Diana had spent the night at Coleherne Court in her flat.

Soon after this, Lady Diana happened to tell a sympathetic neighbour in Coleherne Court: 'The whole thing has got out of control . . . I'm not so much bored as miserable. Everywhere I go there is someone there . . . If I go to a restaurant or just out shopping in the supermarket, there they are, trying to take photographs.' The neighbour happened to be a freelance journalist, Dunae Brooks.

By now, the press's pursuit of Lady Diana had reached an unacceptable level. Her telephone number was still in the telephone book and pressmen were no respectors of privacy, ringing her flat at all hours of the day and night. Lady Diana's mother, Mrs Shand Kydd, wrote to *The Times*, and in a letter published on Tuesday, 2 December, she asked the editors of Fleet Street 'whether in the execution of their jobs, they consider it necessary or fair to harass my daughter from dawn until well after dusk?' Buckingham Palace also complained about the way the press were mistreating Lady Diana and that it 'degraded the whole trade of journalism'. Sixty MPs accused the media of 'hounding' Lady Diana and called upon those responsible 'to have more concern for individual privacy.' The newspapers duly published this but their representatives continued to mount a daily watch on Coleherne Court. In the meantime, Lady Diana and her three flatmates had worked out a system of decoys between them so that she could come and go without too much trouble.

During this time, the Prince of Wales was in India and Nepal on an official tour. He left Heathrow on 23 November in an RAF VC10 for Delhi, without Lord Mountbatten, the last Viceroy of India, who should have accompanied the Prince but who had been assassinated in 1979. The pressmen covering the tour were more anxious for hints of an engagement than to report on the official happenings. When asked what he thought of the Taj Mahal, the Prince of Wales replied: 'It was a marvellous idea to build something so wonderful . . . to someone one loved so very much.' According to an Indian legend, any man who visits the Taj Mahal as a bachelor will return with a wife. The Prince refused to be drawn by the very obvious question asked by an Indian reporter: 'When you return, will you bring your wife?' After a moment's reflection the Prince replied: 'I might take up the Muslim religion and have lots of wives. That would be much more fun.'

Prince Charles spent the New Year of 1980–1 with the Royal Family at Sandringham surrounded by the press.

When he returned to England in mid-December, Prince Charles drove to join the rest of the Royal Family at Windsor for Christmas. It was after Christmas that the Prince and the Royal Family went to Sandringham for the New Year holiday. Lady Diana spent Christmas at Althorp and soon afterwards returned to London, where she saw the New Year in with friends. But the next day she drove to Sandringham, exciting further speculation by the ubiquitous press. The Royal Family had themselves been under close surveillance by reporters and photographers since before Christmas and were displeased at the invasion of their privacy. Buckingham Palace issued a statement saying: 'The Queen is very disturbed. Sandringham is a completely private house and the family come and go. They always have a private holiday and are left alone as they are not carrying out any official engagements at all. Now they can hardly move without being photographed.' The Prince of Wales, resorting to untypical sarcasm, shouted to pressmen: 'A very happy New Year, and to your editors a particularly nasty one!'

Lady Diana proved more difficult to find. With her friends acting as decoys and car-drivers when necessary, she was able to slip away to Highgrove to

Left: Prince Charles cycling to join Lady Diana for breakfast at Nicholas Gaselee's house in Upper Lambourn

Right: Prince Charles and his gun dog, Harvey

lunch with the Prince a week after her Sandringham visit. They met at dawn the next day at the stables of the Prince's trainer, Nicholas Gaselee, in Upper Lambourn, and the Prince rode his horse, Allibar, before returning to London for the funeral of Princess Alice, Countess of Athlone.

The weekend of 9–11 January was spent by Lady Diana at Althorp where, in search of some privacy and some time to herself, she walked alone around the estate. Prince Charles spent that weekend on his own at Highgrove. They were together again the following Wednesday at Sandringham, Lady Diana arriving the evening before with the Duchess of Kent. Once again the press failed to notice her departure. The following morning they followed the Prince of Wales in his Land Rover when he went to collect Harvey, his yellow labrador, from the head-keeper while Lady Diana slipped away from the house, unnoticed, in a borrowed car and drove to her flat in London. The Prince later told the foiled pressmen: 'There's no one here. I wish you would all go away! The Queen would be very pleased if you did!'

A week later the Prince of Wales was in Switzerland, skiing at Klosters and staying in a chalet taken by Charles Palmer-Tomkinson and his wife, Patty. European pressmen, on the look-out for Lady Diana, invaded the ski-slopes. But she never appeared. The Prince returned to England, looking fit and tanned, on 3 February, and managed to meet Lady Diana without attracting any attention.

On Thursday, 5 February, the Prince joined HMS *Invincible*, the Navy's latest aircraft carrier, in the Channel for manoeuvres. He returned to London that evening and dined with Lady Diana in his apartments at Buckingham Palace.

It was after dinner that night that the Prince of Wales proposed to her. She was flying to Australia the following day and the Prince of Wales advised her not to give her answer immediately but to think it over. Lady Diana, however, accepted at once. 'I never had any doubts about it,' she said later.

She returned to Coleherne Court and the next morning told her flatmates; they were delighted. They opened a bottle of champagne in celebration before going to work. Lady Diana packed for her long-planned holiday with her mother and step-father on their sheep property in Australia.

Later that night, Lady Diana travelled with her mother and step-father on a scheduled Qantas flight, QF2 to Sydney. Her secret departure was a well-organized operation and only the captain of the 747 jet knew the identity of his extra passenger, who

sat beside the Shand Kydds. It was Lady Diana's first visit to Australia. Undetected, they reached the Shand Kydd sheep-station at Yass, next door to a large property owned by the newspaper magnate, Rupert Murdoch, owner also of the *News of the World*, *The Sun*, and *The Times*. For a day and a half Lady Diana relaxed in a completely new environment with her mother and Peter Shand Kydd. But the Australian reporters learned the whereabouts of the Prince of Wales' *fiancée*. The press in England, having lost her, were desperately telephoning Mrs Shand Kydd enquiring whether Lady Diana was with her. Naturally, her mother denied this. Then one morning the Australian press descended upon the sheep-station in a helicopter chartered by a local television station – circling over the property before eventually landing by the house. Reporters and photographers invaded the unprotected farmland.

The Shand Kydds were besieged. They sought the help of some Australian friends, who enabled them to escape to a beach house on the coast of New South Wales lent to them by a friend. Here, for seven days, Lady Diana, her mother and step-father, enjoyed at last a relaxing holiday, catching up on lost sleep, swimming and surfing off a near-deserted beach. The few who knew where they were told no one. However, the suspense of not knowing when a photographer would suddenly appear, from the sky, the sea, or the land, eventually cast a shadow on the holiday. Mrs Shand Kydd decided that Lady Diana should return to England; she was smuggled out of Australia and flew back home.

The next report that appeared in the newspapers, on Friday, 20 February, was that Lady Diana was back in her flat in London – where she had been for two days. Later that day she drove to Highgrove. The next morning she went with the Prince of Wales to Nicholas Gaselee's stables at Upper Lambourn. The Prince was scheduled to ride his eleven-year-old horse, Allibar, the following afternoon in the Cavalry Hunters Chase at Chepstow and this was a rare chance to 'ride out' at the morning exercise on the Mandown Gallops on the Lambourn Downs. Lady Diana watched as he cantered seven furlongs. Afterwards, the Prince was walking Allibar home when suddenly the horse shuddered and staggered. Prince Charles at once dismounted but the horse collapsed and died from a heart attack. A stable lad who was present said that the Prince 'would not leave the horse until the vet arrived and certified that it was dead.' Lady Diana left the Gaselees' house in the back of a Land Rover, with a coat over her head, and returned to London. The Prince of Wales left for Swansea. Both were very upset. It was a grim-faced Prince who that afternoon received the freedom of the City of Swansea on behalf of the Regiment of Wales. He returned that night to Highgrove.

It was on Saturday, 21 February, that the Prince of

Left: Prince Charles with Allibar on 20 February 1981, the day before the horse died

Right: Lady Diana

Wales telephoned Earl Spencer and asked him for his daughter's hand in marriage. That consent was readily given. On Sunday morning he went alone to church in Tetbury. He sat in a box pew immediately below the pulpit, and afterwards invited the vicar, the Reverend Michael Sherwood, back to Highgrove for a glass of sherry. Later that afternoon he drove back to Buckingham Palace. It was during the evening of Sunday, 22 February, that it was decided the engagement should be announced the following Tuesday. Michael Shea, the Queen's press secretary, was recalled from Norway during the night.

On Monday, 23 February, the Prince travelled to Portsmouth to visit HMS *Bronington*, the mine-hunter he had commanded for ten months in 1976; he lunched in the tiny ward-room. Afterwards he returned to London and was back at Buckingham Palace at about 5.15 p.m., just as Lady Diana, after hastily packing a suitcase, left Coleherne Court in her red Mini Metro with her flatmate, Carolyn Pride. She dropped Carolyn off at South Kensington and drove on to St James's Palace to collect her sister, Lady Jane. The two then drove to Buckingham Palace, where Lady Diana parked her car at the end of the 'Visitors Cars Only' line in the Palace forecourt before going inside to join the Prince and the Earl and Countess Spencer for a celebratory drink. Later the Prince and Lady Diana dined with Robert and Lady Jane Fellowes at the flat of her grandmother, Lady Fermoy, in Eaton Square. A toast was drunk to the future happiness of the Prince of Wales and the Lady Diana Spencer. The following day the world would know that they were engaged.

Right: Prince Charles and Lady Diana at Balmoral with the Prince's gun dog, Harvey, in May 1981

A Horoscope of Prince Charles and Lady Diana

Prince Charles was born when the Sun was moving through Scorpio, one of the 'Water-Element' zodiac-signs, and at a time of night when the 'Fire-Element' sign Leo was on the eastern horizon of his birthplace. He has a strong character and is a basically self-reliant, courageous man with a keen sense of his responsibilities to his family, the nation and the Commonwealth. Leo gives him a natural capacity for leadership, as well as self-respect, a natural sense of dignity – and integrity. Like the majority of people with Leo prominent in their chart, he has personal magnetism (all the more so because of his Scorpio sun sign); and he has the deep feelings, the need to love and to be loved, the desire for emotional security in his close relationships, inherent in anyone with his particular horoscope pattern.

His horoscope is one which has very close, harmonious links with that of his bride. She, too, has the Sun in a 'Water' sign (Cancer), so they are well in tune with each other emotionally; both are very intuitive, and so conscious of each other's thoughts and feelings that there is little need for speech between them to add to mutual understanding. Her Ascendant sign is a 'Fire' one, Sagittarius – which harmonizes well with his Leo rising sign; this makes for a mutually stimulating relationship. Another especially important link between them is that of the Prince's Moon in Taurus (where Lady Diana has Venus).

Lady Diana is a typical Cancerian girl in that she has the deep-rooted attachment to home and family associated with this sign; her father says of her that 'she's very practical and down to earth, and a very good housewife', and her horoscope corroborates this. Moreover, as she has the Sun in the partnership area of her birthchart, this indicates that she will devote herself wholeheartedly to her husband's interests and aims.

The horoscopes of the Prince and Lady Diana indicate that they have much in common so far as their tastes are concerned; the Prince is well known as an all-round sportsman, and with Sagittarius for her rising sign Lady Diana shares his love of active, energetic outdoor pursuits. His chart indicates that he will be a very affectionate and conscientious father to his children; and as Cancer is the sign of motherhood it's not surprising that Lady Diana confided to a teacher, while at finishing school in Switzerland, that her aim was to marry for love and bring up a family of her own. Both will take particular pleasure in furnishing their homes; both will be provident in handling money matters, and their homes will be run on economical rather than extravagant lines.

There is a high-spirited side to Lady Diana's nature; this again is due to the 'Sagittarian Element' in her chart which also accounts for her keen sense of humour. In fact, their mutual sense of humour and the invigorating effect they have on each other will make it all the easier for them to cope with the rigours they will be subjected to in carrying out their public duties.

Lady Diana is a very healthy girl; both her own and her husband's horoscopes indicate that they will have several very healthy children. The firstborn will probably be a boy (and also, very probably, arrive late in 1982 or during the first half of 1983). Eventually, they should have three, or possibly four offspring.

When Prince Charles becomes king, he will be very popular. His bride has already revealed another characteristic shown in her horoscope – the capacity to establish a close rapport with the public at large. She will take a particularly keen interest in those public organizations which are concerned with the welfare of children and the elderly.

Katina

CHAPTER 10

The Weeks before the Wedding

For Lady Diana, whose way of life changed overnight after her engagement to Prince Charles became official, the following day, Wednesday, 25 February, was indicative of how her future would be spent. She awoke early in a royal residence, and after breakfast she was driven from Clarence House to Buckingham Palace in Prince Charles's Ford Granada estate car. The driver was Chief Inspector Paul Officer, who with Chief Inspector Maclean had been assigned the task of guarding the Prince's *fiancée*, along with two other officers; between them they would protect and accompany the Prince and future Princess of Wales wherever they went in public. At the Palace, Lady Diana was briefly reunited with the Prince before he left at 8.45 a.m. for a series of engagements that would take him to Scotland and keep them apart until Friday. She then began reading the thousands of telegrams and letters of congratulation that had already arrived.

Later that morning, she was driven by Chief Inspector Officer to Coleherne Court to pack the last of her more personal possessions before leaving the flat that had been her home for nearly two years. Outside, before she returned to Clarence House, she paused to greet the pressmen who had dogged her for six months.

In the event, Lady Diana stayed at Clarence House for only a few days, moving after that to a family flat in Pimlico. She was also provided with a suite of rooms in Buckingham Palace, where she might stay and more conveniently take part in the many discussions, dress-fittings and preparations for her forthcoming marriage.

Mrs Shand Kydd returned to London from Australia on Thursday, 26 February. Reporters and photographers surrounded her at Heathrow Airport. She told them something about her holiday with her daughter in Australia and added: 'Of course we talked about Diana's future – I would be a very abnormal mother if we hadn't . . . I'm delighted about the engagement and I'm very proud of my daughter. I'm sure she can cope and will learn very quickly.' She and Lady Diana dined that evening with Lady Jane and Robert Fellowes at Kensington Palace.

On Saturday and Sunday, Prince Charles and Lady Diana spent their first weekend together after the engagement was announced, staying at Cholmondeley Castle, Cheshire, the home of Lord and Lady Cholmondeley. The Prince rode with the Cheshire Hunt, and on Sunday, 1 March, St David's Day, the couple attended a service in the Castle chapel.

After their return to London, the wedding and other arrangements occupied much of their attention. Thousands of congratulatory letters and telegrams had to be answered among other matters. Lady Diana acquired her own, as yet, unofficial private secretary, a diplomat, Oliver Everett, formerly Prince Charles's assistant private secretary.

On Tuesday, 3 March, it was announced that the marriage would take place in St Paul's Cathedral, not in Westminster Abbey as many had expected. That evening Prince Charles and his *fiancée*, on their first night out together since their engagement, paid a private visit to the opera. They sat in the royal box at Covent Garden and watched an international cast, headed by the American soprano, Grace Bumbry, sing Meyerbeer's opera, *L'Africaine*. Their first *official* public appearance together was on Monday, 9 March, when they attended a charity gala of verse and music at the Goldsmiths' Hall in the City of London. At a reception afterwards they met Princess Grace of Monaco. Lady Diana's dress, a low-cut, strapless, black silk taffeta ballgown, created a small sensation. Some eyebrows were raised; pictures of her in *Time* magazine in Iran had her bare shoulders blacked out.

The following day, it was announced by the Palace that David and Elizabeth Emanuel, who had

Prince Charles and Lady Diana attended a recital in aid of the Royal Opera House Development Appeal at Goldsmiths' Hall in London on 9 March 1981. This was their first official function together.

designed the black ballgown, had been chosen to design and make the wedding-dress. Lady Diana's choice of the Emanuels was a break with established fashion-houses and tradition and indicated not only her independence and sense of fashion, but also the likelihood that the Princess of Wales would set styles of her own in the years to come.

Prince Charles provided a different picture when on Friday, 13 March, he went steeplechasing at Sandown and fell off his horse, Good Prospect, at the eighteenth fence. Five days later, at Cheltenham on Tuesday (St Patrick's and Gold Cup Day), he came unstuck at the tenth fence in the Kim Muir Memorial Challenge Cup. Although he bloodied his nose both times and was shaken by the falls, his pride was hurt more than anything. He might have been injured, and some concern was expressed in the Palace and by the press about the advisability of the Prince pursuing this activity, particularly in the weeks before the wedding. In the 1920s the previous Prince of Wales, later Edward VIII, had a series of falls in point-to-points and when riding under national hunt rules. He broke his collar-bone in 1926, and, although he had many winners, he sold all his horses three years later to please his family and pacify the press. The night after Prince Charles fell at Cheltenham, he and Lady Diana attended a banquet at Buckingham Palace in honour of the President of Nigeria. The following evening, the couple were entertained by Lord (Sam) Vestey at Stowell Park, his 4,500-acre estate near Cheltenham racecourse.

Lady Diana and Prince Charles were back in Cheltenham on Friday, 27 March, on an official visit to the Headquarters of the Gloucestershire Police, who would be responsible for the safeguarding of Highgrove. As they were about to leave the town, in a red Wessex helicopter piloted by the Prince, a sixth-form schoolboy in the cheering crowd unofficially presented Lady Diana with a single daffodil and asked: 'May I kiss the hand of my future Queen?'

'Yes, you may,' she replied, and added as he did so – 'You'll never live this down!'

Further approval of the bride-to-be was officially given at Buckingham Palace that afternoon. At a special meeting, in the White Drawing Room, the Privy Council under its President, Lord Soames, asked the Queen to give her formal consent to the marriage – in accordance with the Royal Marriage Act of 1772, which states that no royal descendants of George II can marry without the monarch's permission. It was only the second meeting of the Council to be attended by Prince Charles and the first time that the press were allowed to take pictures of the Council. Afterwards, the Queen posed for her first photographs with her future daughter-in-law and her eldest son.

Royal duties separated the couple two days later. On Sunday, 29 March, the Prince flew to New Zealand, to begin a five-week tour that would take him on to Australia, Venezuela and America. He and Lady Diana parted on the rainy, wind-swept tarmac at Heathrow Airport. Before he climbed the gangway of the RAF VC10 he grasped her arm and kissed her on each cheek. She stood at the terminal and watched with tears in her eyes as the plane taxied away.

The first details of the wedding arrangements were announced by the Palace on Tuesday, 31 March, as Prince Charles arrived in Wellington, New Zealand. During the tour, despite a crowded, active schedule which allowed him little relaxation apart from a game of polo, he telephoned Lady Diana every day. In Britain, the Lord Chamberlain, Lord Maclean, issued a three-page ruling about wedding souvenirs, which were to be in good taste: the Royal Arms or royal photographs should not appear on articles such as T-shirts. The souvenir industry, spurred on by the millions of pounds to be made, raced ahead undaunted manufacturing well over 2,000 kinds of memorabilia, taking care, however, to insure their products for over £20 million against any cancellation or postponement of the wedding. The last major royal event that was suddenly postponed was the coronation of Edward VII – because of his operation for appendicitis a week before the event.

Soon details of the bridesmaids and wedding cake were released while Lady Diana, much occupied with her own arrangements, made trips to dress designers, dress shops and milliners, extending her wardrobe and choosing her trousseau. She found time to see *They're Playing Our Song* at the Shaftesbury Theatre, on 20 April, accompanied by the Hon. Nicholas Soames and his *fiancée*, and she visited the Queen at Windsor the following day on Her Majesty's fifty-fifth birthday. Prince Charles was now in Australia and involved in a very full programme of visits and events. As if in hopeful expectation of one day being Governor General, in most of his speeches he referred to Lady Diana, apologizing for her absence and saying he hoped they would return to Australia together.

After visiting Venezuela and meeting President Reagan in Washington, he flew in an RAF VC10 back to Britain on Sunday, 3 May. He landed at RAF Lossiemouth and drove to Balmoral where Lady Diana was waiting. They were reunited at Craigowan. Her British Airways flight that day from Heathrow to Aberdeen had been beset by thunderstorms and the plane was struck by lightning.

Storms of another sort were brewing in Australia, West Germany and Britain over the claim that telephone calls which the Prince had made from Government House in Canberra to his mother and

Above: The Queen in Privy Council on 27 March 1981 gave her formal consent to the marriage of the Prince of Wales to Lady Diana Spencer.

Right: After the meeting of the Privy Council the Queen posed in the Music Room at Buckingham Palace for her first official photographs with the Prince and Lady Diana.

fiancée had been tapped, taped and transcribed and would be published in a West German magazine. On Wednesday, 6 May, the Prince and Lady Diana, who were enjoying a brief salmon-fishing holiday on the Balmoral estate, obtained a High Court injunction preventing the tapes from being published in Britain. But when a transcript of the alleged taped conversations was seen, it was realized that the tapes were false and a hoax, and the Prince's solicitors, Farrer and Company, announced on Thursday: 'We are quite satisfied that the telephone conversations of which this [material] purports to be a transcript did not take place.'

With all that unpleasantness out of the way, Prince Charles and Lady Diana returned to London on Friday, 8 May, and on Saturday visited Broadlands, the Hampshire home of Lord Romsey, where they planted a tree and opened the Mountbatten Exhibition. The Royal Family's season of summer engagements was now in full swing and Lady Diana's name began to appear on Court Circulars, while her summer outfits and hats invited comment and admiration. On 14 May, when the President of Ghana

lunched at Windsor Castle with the Queen and the Duke of Edinburgh, Lady Diana and Prince Charles were also present. During the afternoon, Lady Diana, with the Duke of Edinburgh, watched the Queen, escorted by Prince Charles, ceremoniously present new Colours to the 1st Battalion, Welsh Guards. Afterwards, she attended a garden party given for 2,000 guests at Victoria Barracks, Windsor.

Lady Diana's next public appearance with her *fiancé* was in Tetbury, near Highgrove, on Friday, 22 May, when they attended a dedication service in the parish church. They then walked through the town, among much enthusiastic applause, to Tetbury hospital, where the Prince opened a new operating theatre.

Prince Charles's official engagements in the weeks that followed often took him out of London. During this time Lady Diana visited Princess Anne in St Mary's Hospital, Paddington where on 15 May she had given birth to her second child, Zara. On Thursday, 4 June, Lady Diana attended the wedding of the Hon. Nicholas Soames and Catherine Weatherall at St Margaret's Church, Westminster. Prince Charles was best man. The next wedding Lady Diana and the Prince would be present at would be their own.

The couple attended two lavish banquets the following week: one given by the Queen at Buckingham Palace to honour the State Visit of King Khaled of Saudi Arabia and the other by the King at Claridge's. On Thursday, 11 June, the Prince and Lady Diana went to St Paul's Cathedral to hear the music they had chosen for the wedding and for a rehearsal of the service. They also lunched with the Archbishop of Canterbury and discussed the final arrangements, deciding that Lady Diana would vow to 'love, honour and cherish' but not 'obey'. On Saturday, 13 June, Lady Diana stood with the Queen and other members of the Royal Family on the balcony of Buckingham Palace when the Queen took the salute at 1 p.m. during a fly-past of RAF jets after the Queen's Birthday Parade.

After the weekend Lady Diana, as 'a lady of a Knight Companion of the Order', attended the Order of the Garter service of thanksgiving in St George's Chapel, Windsor, on Monday, 15 June. The following day the Royal Ascot races began. Each day of the meeting she rode with the Royal Family in a landau down the course. On the Wednesday, Prince Charles flew by Concorde to New York for a gala performance given there by the Royal Ballet. The week ended with a birthday ball for 600 guests at Windsor Castle, given in belated celebration of Prince Andrew's twenty-first birthday and of the Duke of Edinburgh's sixtieth. It meant yet another ballgown for Lady Diana – as did a soirée at the Royal Academy of Arts, Piccadilly on the 23rd, and the Gala Première at the Odeon, Leicester Square, of the James Bond film, *For Your Eyes Only*, on the 24th. On Saturday, 27 June, she went with Prince Charles to the Military Musical Pageant at Wembley Stadium.

It must sometimes have been tiring for Lady Diana to be ever looking her best and smiling at all and sundry. Accustomed as she was to royalty, she was still a commoner and unaccustomed to the weight of royal protocol and responsibility; and the stares and

Left: Lady Diana with the Royal Family on the balcony of Buckingham Palace after the Queen's Birthday Parade on 13 June 1981. The next time Lady Diana would appear on the balcony would be with Prince Charles after their wedding.

Right: Mr and Mrs Peter Shand Kydd, Viscount Althorp and Lady Fermoy leaving for the dinner-party at Buckingham Palace on Monday, 27 July 1981.

cries of thousands of people, their eyes all looking at *her*, at times must have been a burden for a modest young girl. But at Highgrove, on Tuesday, 30 June, when Prince Charles gave a garden party for hundreds of tenants of the Duchy of Cornwall, she was happy and very relaxed. Her happiness extended next day to her birthday – she was twenty – when there was a private party in the evening for her family and close friends. Prince Charles returned to London in time for the celebration after opening an exhibition in Newcastle-upon-Tyne. It was a very different birthday from that spent a year before in Coleherne Court with Virginia Pitman – when, with the other two flatmates away, the girls shared a simple birthday supper in the flat.

On 2 July, Lady Diana saw the men's singles semi-finals at Wimbledon from the royal box. She also attended Wimbledon with her sisters on the Friday and Saturday and watched the triumphs of Chris Lloyd and John McEnroe. During the next week, she saw very little of Prince Charles as he fulfilled a heavy schedule of engagements in Scotland. But on Sunday, 12 July, he was back in England, taking part in a sponsored charity show-jumping event for Stoke Mandeville Hospital at Ascot racecourse. He also played polo for *Les Diables Bleus* in the British Open Championships at Windsor and Cowdray Park.

A week before the wedding, on 22 July, two stamps were issued, 14p and 25p, commemorating the event. That morning Lady Diana had a final fitting for her wedding-dress, at the Emanuel's salon in Brook Street, before attending a wedding rehearsal in St Paul's at 6 p.m. Two hours later Prince Charles had a small stag-night dinner-party at White's Club in St James's. The next day the Prince and his *fiancée* were interviewed for television at Buckingham Palace by Angela Rippon and Andrew Gardner. On the Sunday he played polo for England II at Windsor against Spain. On Monday night the Queen gave a dinner-party at Buckingham Palace for the Royal Family's closest friends and wedding guests which was followed by a reception and a dance.

The night before the wedding there was a spectacular firework display in Hyde Park. Before a crowd that numbered more than half a million, Prince Charles, watched by the Queen, the Duke of Edinburgh, members of the Royal Family and many royal and distinguished wedding guests, lit the first of a nationwide chain of 101 beacons and bonfires at 10.08 p.m. The firework display that followed, costing £80,000, was accompanied by music from the massed bands of the Household Musicians, with singing by the Morrison Orpheus Choir and the Choir of the Welsh Guards, and salvoes from the guns of the King's Troop, Royal Horse Artillery. It was the biggest display of its kind in Britain for over two hundred years. Lady Diana, however, spent the evening before her wedding at Clarence House.

The weeks of preparation and pageantry were over. The next time she and the Prince of Wales would meet would be in St Paul's Cathedral, exchanging vows before the Queen, their families and friends, and before the eyes of the largest television audience in the world.

CHAPTER 11

The Wedding

The day dawned calm and bright. The sun, arising at 5.20 a.m. in a warm golden haze, found central London strangely still, even for a Bank Holiday: the streets between Buckingham Palace and St Paul's Cathedral were largely devoid of traffic and littered with people; thousands had bedded down on the pavements, some since Sunday, beneath banners, flags, pennants and baskets of flowers. As the sun rose the sleepers awoke, struggling to their feet, and as new arrivals flocked in, they manned their chosen vantage-points at the barriers along The Mall, in Trafalgar Square, the Strand, Fleet Street and Ludgate Hill. Excited chatter and the sounds of transistor radios replaced the usual bustle of the awakening city.

Independent Television's coverage of the wedding began at 7.30 a.m.; BBC Television's began fifteen minutes later. By 10 a.m. more than 250 million listeners around the world would have tuned in to BBC Radio on the World Service, joining those switched on to Radios 1, 2, and 4 – Radio 3 confined itself to classical music all day – and those who were listening to the Independent Radio stations. By then, well over 700 million people in seventy nations would be watching BBC Television's biggest ever live Outside Broadcast, costing £½ million and involving sixty cameras and 350 staff. Independent Television's operation was as large. Extensive foreign coverage by the mass media also ensured that the wedding would be seen and heard that day by a worldwide audience of more than 1,000 million people.

In Clarence House, the bride arose early and began preparing herself for the marriage ceremony, assisted by a make-up artist, her hairdresser and couturiers, and supported by her mother and sisters. She arranged herself in her wedding-dress, which would soon become the avid focus of millions of womens' eyes.

Lady Diana Spencer led by her father up the aisle of the nave in St Paul's Cathedral at the beginning of her marriage service on 29 July 1981.

The total cost of the seven attendants' dresses and costumes was some £500 more than the value of the bride's dress, veil, train and shoes, reputed to be £2,300. The estimated overall cost of the wedding was some £½ million. About £60,000 of this would be paid by the Queen and Prince Charles. 'Thank God, I don't have to pay for it!' Earl Spencer said. More than half of the total sum was spent on security arrangements: about 3,500 policemen were on special duty that day, as well as 1,950 officers and other ranks from all three armed services, who lined the processional route. They took up their positions by 9.30 a.m., and the policemen, facing the crowd, as early as 6 a.m.

The official weather forecast for the London area had promised 'a bright start to the day; although some increase in the cloud is likely, there will still be a good deal of sunshine; it will stay dry and warm . . .' And so it proved to be. If the weather had been inclement, Buckingham Palace had an alternative fleet of closed coaches standing by.

By 9.30 a.m., the jostling crowds were in an unusual fever of anticipation and patriotic excitement. Packed ten deep on the pavements and decked with cameras, periscopes and union jacks, they eagerly observed and cheered every activity before them. At St Paul's, the 2,600 wedding guests had already begun to arrive, slowly pacing through the West Door into the brilliant interior, showing their seating cards to ushers. Their large white, gilt-edged invitations, bearing the legend: 'The Lord Chamberlain is Commanded by the Queen and the Duke of Edinburgh to invite . . .' had been received four months ago. The majority of the guests were servants of the Crown and State: diplomats, politicians, civil servants, senior members of the services, heads of industry, local government officials, and over 200 members of the Queen's staff from Sandringham, Balmoral, and Windsor. There were over 160 foreign presidents, prime ministers, and their wives, including Mrs Nancy Reagan, the wife of the President of

The crowds lining the route to St Paul's – many people used periscopes for a better view.

the United States of America. European royalty – including the Kings and Queens of the Belgians and of Sweden, the King of Norway, the Queen of the Netherlands, the Grand Duke and Duchess of Luxembourg, and Princess Grace of Monaco – were far outnumbered by the monarchs of Africa, the Middle East and Asia. All the closer friends of the bride and groom were invited, including several of the groom's former associates in the services; some, friends of the Prince and of Mrs Shand Kydd, came from as far away as Australia.

The large numbers of wedding guests were increased by the many officials, technicians, and performers attending the service: by musicians, choristers and ushers, by television crews and security men, and by the clergy. The thirty boys and eighteen men of the Choir of St Paul's Cathedral were augmented by the Gentlemen and Children of Her Majesty's Chapels Royal, as well as by the amateurs of the 200-strong Bach Choir, with whom their president, Prince Charles, had sometimes sang. The large programme of music would be played by the twelve State Trumpeters of the Household Cavalry, the eighteen Fanfare Trumpeters of the Royal Military School of Music, Kneller Hall, and by the English Chamber Orchestra, the Orchestra of the Royal Opera House, Covent Garden, and the Philharmonia Orchestra. The Prince is patron of all three orchestras.

Most of the congregation were required to be seated by 10 a.m., an hour before the service began. In the interim, they listened to organ music played by the cathedral organist, Christopher Dearnley, and his assistant, John Scott.

Between 10.00 and 10.25, heads of state and foreign royalty began arriving. They were led to their seats at the forefront of the congregation, below the central dome. At 10.15 junior members of the Royal Family appeared, having been driven in limousines from St James's Palace. They included Lord and Lady Harewood, the Duke of Fife, the Marchioness of Cambridge, and the Duke and Duchess of Beaufort. The congregation stood as an eccleciastical procession moved from the north aisle into the choir, led by a virger, cross-bearer, taperers, choristers, minor canons and representatives of four different churches, who would give the marriage service its ecumenical flavour. These included the Speaker of the House of Commons, the Rt. Hon. George Thomas, a Methodist; the Moderator of the Free Church Federal Council, the Rev. Morris West; the Roman Catholic Archbishop of Westminster, Cardinal Hume; and the Moderator of the Church of Scotland, the Rt. Rev. Andrew Doig.

At 10.20, Mrs Frances Shand Kydd, her husband, Peter, and her son, Viscount Althorp, aged seventeen – who had left Clarence House by car at 10.10 – arrived at St Paul's. Mrs Shand Kydd wore a dress of cornflower blue chiffon and a matching hat. She was greeted by her son-in-law, Robert Fellowes, who escorted her up the nave where she took her place in the front row to the left of the central dais, joining her mother, Lady Fermoy, her two other daughters and their husbands. The bride's three flatmates sat together right at the front of the congregation. Lady Spencer, dressed in blue, sat a few rows behind them with her youngest son.

At 10.25 the cars bringing the foreign crowned heads from Buckingham Palace began to arrive, preceding the appearance at the West Door at 10.30 of the bridesmaids and pages, who had left Clarence House by car ten minutes before.

The bridesmaids and pages were sons or daughters of Prince Charles's relatives and friends. The youngest bridesmaid, five-year-old Miss Clementine Hambro, had also been one of Lady Diana's charges at the Pimlico kindergarten. She is daughter of Mr and Mrs Richard Hambro and great-grand-daughter of Sir Winston Churchill. The other attendants were six-year-old Miss Catherine Cameron, daughter of Mr Donald Cameron of Locheil and Lady Cecil Cameron; Sarah Jane Gaselee, aged ten, daughter of Mr and Mrs Nicholas Gaselee; fourteen-year-old Miss India Hicks, daughter of interior designer, David Hicks and Lady Pamela, younger daughter of Lord Mountbatten; Lady Sarah Armstrong-Jones, daughter of Princess Margaret and Lord Snowdon; Edward van Cutsem, aged eight, son of Mr and Mrs Hugh van Cutsem; and the youngest son of the Duke and Duchess of Kent, eleven-year-old Lord Nicholas Windsor. They assembled within the West Door, as the Dean of St Paul's, the Very Rev. Alan Webster, and Chapter, with the Bishop of London, and the Archbishop of Canterbury, the Most Rev. and Rt. Hon. Robert Runcie, positioned themselves to the right of the entrance. The Archbishop wore a new gleaming blue and silver cope. At 10.36 the Lord Mayor of London, Alderman Sir Ronald Gardner-Thorpe, arrived.

Meanwhile, the thronging crowds outside Buckingham Palace at last had great cause to cheer and wave their flags as, at 10.22, the Queen's Carriage Procession of eight landaus left the Palace. It was preceded by the Sovereign's Escort. The first carriage, an open Semi-State Postillion Landau drawn by four Grey horses, contained the Queen and the Duke of Edinburgh, and swept across the Palace

The Queen and Prince Philip travelling to St Paul's Cathedral for the wedding of Prince Charles and Lady Diana Spencer.

The Queen Mother with Prince Edward in the second carriage of the Queen's Carriage Procession from Buckingham Palace to St Paul's Cathedral

Princess Anne and Princess Margaret followed the Queen Mother's carriage in a State Landau, with Captain Mark Phillips and Viscount Linley.

forecourt into the banner-lined Mall. The Queen wore a finely pleated dress of pale aquamarine crêpe de chine; a thin rug covered her knees. The Duke of Edinburgh was in the uniform of an Admiral of the Fleet. In the second carriage sat Queen Elizabeth the Queen Mother and Prince Edward; in the third were Princess Anne, Captain Mark Phillips, Princess Margaret and her son, Viscount Linley. The other five carriages contained the royal families of the Gloucesters, Kents and Ogilvys with their children, and chief members of the Royal Household.

At 10.30, the two-carriage procession of the Prince of Wales, preceded by an escort of the Life Guards, left the Palace. The bridegroom, a Commander in the Royal Navy, wore the Navy's No. 1 ceremonial dress uniform and a blue Garter sash; he sat with his brother, Prince Andrew, in the 1902 State Postillion Landau. Prince Andrew wore the uniform of a midshipman of the Royal Navy. In the second carriage were members of Prince Charles's Household. All the coachmen, postillions, and footmen wore State Liveries of scarlet and gold – except for the postillions on the bridegroom's carriage who wore Ascot Liveries.

The Prince of Wales' Carriage Procession and that of the Queen reached St Paul's Cathedral twenty minutes later. There the occupants of the royal carriages ascended the steps to the West Door and paused to re-group themselves before walking up the nave, their processions being led by two gentlemen ushers and prefaced by a change in the organ music. The Queen and the Duke of Edinburgh were preceded by the eighteen senior members of the Royal Family, by the Queen Mother, by the Lord Mayor, bearing the Pearl Sword given to the City of London by Elizabeth I, the Lord Steward (the Duke of Northumberland), and by the Lord Chamberlain. They were followed by members of the Royal Household. When the Queen reached her chair she acknowledged with a smile the bride's family. During the bridegroom's procession, the organist played the 'Trumpet Tune' by Purcell. The Prince of Wales, with his brothers as 'supporters' – there was no best man – set off before the tune began. He was preceded by two admirals acting as gentlemen ushers and followed by three members of his staff. Throughout the long walk he glanced to left and right, smiling delightedly at friends he recognized. As the Prince turned into the Dean's Aisle, the south aisle, he must have heard the cheering outside that greeted the arrival of his bride.

Lady Diana Spencer left Clarence House with her father, Earl Spencer, at 10.37, in the Glass Coach. The

Right: The Prince of Wales with his brother, Prince Andrew, travelled to St Paul's Cathedral for his wedding in the 1902 State Postillion Landau.

The Duchess of Kent with her daughter, Lady Helen Windsor, in the fifth carriage of the Queen's Carriage Procession to St Paul's Cathedral

Princess Alexandra, the Hon. Angus Ogilvy and their children, James and Marina Ogilvy, wave to crowds along the wedding route.

Above: Lady Diana Spencer travelled with her father, Earl Spencer, in the Glass Coach to St Paul's Cathedral for her marriage to the Prince of Wales.

Below: Lady Diana's wedding-dress had a sweeping 25-foot train trimmed with lace. The dress was made of ivory pure silk taffeta with embroidered lace panels at the front and back of the bodice. Both the dress and tulle veil were hand-embroidered with mother-of-pearl sequins and pearls, as were her matching silk slippers. Her veil was kept in place by the Spencer family tiara.

coach, trailed by a limousine in case it broke down, was built in 1910 and bought by George V for his coronation. Drawn by a pair of Bay horses, it was escorted by mounted military and civil police. The bride, blooming in a cloud of tulle, looked enchanting. She carried a bouquet of gardenias, golden roses, orchids, stephanotis, lilies of the valley, freesias, myrtle and veronica, created by the Worshipful Company of Gardeners. She appeared to have fully recovered from the stresses and tensions of the past five months, and in particular from the previous weekend, when after three official engagements in two days, she had shown visible signs of nervous strain. 'It was all too much for her,' said the Prince. But now she seemed quite composed and confident. As she herself confessed: It's taken a bit getting used to the cameras. But it's wonderful to see people's enthusiastic reaction, a mass of smiling faces. It's most rewarding and gives me a tremendous boost.'

The Glass Coach arrived at the Cathedral at 10.56. Lady Sarah Armstrong-Jones and India Hicks helped to spread out the bride's long train, and a stirring fanfare rang out as the bride mounted the steps to the West Door. Her father was supported up the steps by his chauffeur. Within the cathedral entrance, the bride was greeted by the Dean, the Bishop and Archbishop. Her dress and veil were rearranged by the Emanuels as the bridal procession formed. Outside, the cathedral clock struck 11 o'clock.

During the long three-and-a-half minute walk up the nave, the 'Trumpet Voluntary' was played on the organ by Sir David Willcocks. As the bride and her proud father approached the dais under the great

Prince Charles is joined by Lady Diana, on the arm of Earl Spencer, at the dais under the Great Dome of St Paul's at the beginning of their marriage service.

dome, Prince Charles, who had moved to the foot of the dais with his supporters, looked back down the nave. He smiled encouragingly at her as they stepped together onto the dais, moving forward to face the choir and the high altar.

Earl Spencer stood on his daughter's left, stoutly clasping her arm; Prince Andrew and Prince Edward stood to the right of their eldest brother. To the left of the dais were the seven closest members of the bride's family. Opposite them, were the Queen, the Duke of Edinburgh, and the Queen Mother; behind the Queen was Princess Anne, whose baby daughter, Zara, had been christened two days earlier in the private chapel at Windsor Castle. Beside Captain Phillips stood Princess Margaret and her son.

As the final chords of the 'Trumpet Voluntary' reverberated over a scene of extraordinary regal splendour, the programmes containing the Order of the Service were opened and consulted. Now the marriage could begin.

in St Paul's Cathedral
on Wednesday 29th July 1981
at 11.00 a.m.

Before the service, the following music shall be played

Paean .... *Herbert Howells*
Preludio al Vespro di Monteverdi .... *Michael Tippett*
Prelude and Fugue on
a theme of Vittoria .... *Benjamin Britten*
Aria I *and* Toccata
from 'Symphony for Organ' .... *Malcolm Williamson*
Sonata I in G, Op. 28
Allegro maestoso
Allegretto
Andante espressivo
Presto commodo .... *Edward Elgar*
Psalm-Prelude, Set II no. 3
(Psalm 33 v. 3) .... *Herbert Howells*
Andante tranquillo from 'Praeludium' .... *Arthur Bliss*
Trumpet March .... *Geoffrey Bush*
Rhosymedre .... *Ralph Vaughan Williams*

During the Procession of Her Majesty The Queen
Rondeau *from* 'Abdelazar' .... *Henry Purcell*

During the Procession of His Royal Highness The Prince of Wales
Trumpet Tune .... *Henry Purcell*

ORDER OF SERVICE

During the Procession of the Bride, there shall be played

The Trumpet Voluntary (The Prince
of Denmark's March) .... *Jeremiah Clarke*
Organist of St Paul's 1699–1707

Then all shall join in singing
HYMN 170 *(EH)*

Christ is made the sure Foundation,
And the precious Corner-stone,
Who, the two walls underlying
Bound in each, binds both in one,
Holy Sion's help for ever,
And her confidence alone.

To this temple, where we call thee,
Come, O Lord of Hosts, to-day;
With thy wonted loving-kindness
Hear thy people as they pray;
And thy fullest benediction
Shed within its walls for ay.

Here vouchsafe to all thy servants
What they supplicate to gain:
Here to have and hold for ever
Those good things their prayers obtain,
And hereafter in thy glory
With thy blessed ones to reign.

Laud and honour to the Father;
Laud and honour to the Son;
Laud and honour to the Spirit;
Ever Three and ever One:
Consubstantial, co-eternal,
While unending ages run. *Amen.*

Words 7th century trans. J. M. Neale *Music Westminster Abbey Henry Purcell*

THE FORM OF
SOLEMNIZATION OF MATRIMONY

Then shall all be seated, and the Choir shall sing

Let the people praise thee, O God:
yea, let all the people praise thee.

Words from Psalm 67 *Music William Mathias*

Then shall follow
THE LESSON
read by
THE RIGHT HONOURABLE GEORGE THOMAS,
SPEAKER OF THE HOUSE OF COMMONS

I Corinthians 13

All shall remain seated for
THE ADDRESS
by
THE MOST REVEREND AND RIGHT HONOURABLE
ROBERT RUNCIE, M.C., D.D., ARCHBISHOP OF CANTERBURY,
PRIMATE OF ALL ENGLAND AND METROPOLITAN

Then the Choir shall sing
THE ANTHEM

Words Psalm 122.1–3, 6, 7 *Music Charles Parry*

The anthem ended, the congregation shall kneel for
THE PRAYERS

The Lesser Litany shall be sung by the MINOR CANON

Lord, have mercy upon us
Christ, have mercy upon us
Lord, have mercy upon us

V. O Lord, save thy servant, and thy handmaid;
R. Who put their trust in thee.

V. O Lord, send them help from thy holy place;
R. And evermore defend them.

V. Be unto them a tower of strength;
R. From the face of their enemy.

V. O Lord, hear our prayer;
R. And let our cry come unto thee.

Then THE RIGHT REVEREND AND RIGHT HONOURABLE THE LORD COGGAN *shall say*

Heavenly Father, we thank you that in our earthly lives you speak to us of our eternal life: we pray that through their marriage CHARLES and DIANA may know you more clearly, love you more dearly, and follow you more nearly, day by day; through Jesus Christ our Lord. *Amen.*

THE CARDINAL ARCHBISHOP OF WESTMINSTER *shall say*

Almighty God, you send your Holy Spirit to be the life and light of all your people. Open the hearts of these your children to the riches of his grace, that they may bring forth the fruit of the Spirit in love and joy and peace; through Jesus Christ our Lord. *Amen.*

THE MODERATOR OF THE GENERAL ASSEMBLY OF THE CHURCH OF SCOTLAND *shall say*

Heavenly Father, maker of all things, you enable us to share in your work of creation. Bless this couple in the gift and care of children, that their home may be a place of love, security, and truth, and their children grow up to know and love you in your Son Jesus Christ our Lord. *Amen.*

THE REVEREND HARRY WILLIAMS *shall say*

O God, you who are the giver of all happiness because you are the giver of all love, we thank you and praise your name for the love you have given to these your servants, CHARLES PRINCE OF WALES and DIANA PRINCESS OF WALES. Bless and enrich them in their joy; grant that they may continually grow in their understanding and support of one another so that their home may be to them a sanctuary in which they may ever be made new; supply them with the resources they will need to meet the great responsibilities which will fall upon them in their life of service to this kingdom and commonwealth; and when, as all people must, they have to encounter times of hardship and trial, give them the wisdom and strength to bring them through victoriously. We thank you for all they mean to us and will do for us. And, as we rejoice in their happiness, grant us all to see that it is in the service of your self-giving love alone that true happiness can be found, as was shown us by your Son, Jesus Christ our Lord. *Amen.*

Then shall he lead the congregation in saying

THE LORD'S PRAYER

Our Father, who art in heaven, Hallowed be thy Name. Thy Kingdom come. Thy will be done, on earth as it is in heaven. Give us this day our daily bread. And forgive us our trespasses. As we forgive those who trespass against us. And lead us not into temptation; But deliver us from evil. *Amen.*

and continue with

THE BLESSING OF THE COUPLE

Almighty God, the Father of our Lord Jesus Christ, Pour upon you the riches of his grace, sanctify and bless you, that you may please him both in body and soul, and live together in holy love unto your lives' end.

The congregation standing, all shall sing

HYMN 579 *(AMR)*

I vow to thee, my country, all earthly things above,
Entire and whole and perfect, the service of my love:
The love that asks no question, the love that stands the test,
That lays upon the altar the dearest and the best;
The love that never falters, the love that pays the price,
The love that makes undaunted the final sacrifice.

And there's another country, I've heard of long ago,
Most dear to them that love her, most great to them that know;
We may not count her armies, we may not see her King;
Her fortress is a faithful heart, her pride is suffering;
And soul by soul and silently her shining bounds increase,
And her ways are ways of gentleness and all her paths are peace.

Words Cecil Spring-Rice *Music Gustav Holst*

All shall kneel, and THE ARCHBISHOP OF CANTERBURY *shall pronounce*

THE BLESSING

All shall stand to sing

God save our gracious Queen,
Long live our noble Queen,
God save the Queen.
Send her victorious,
Happy and glorious,
Long to reign over us:
God save the Queen.

The choicest gifts in store
On her be pleased to pour,
Long may she reign.
May she defend our laws,
And ever give us cause
To sing with heart and voice,
God save the Queen.

Arr. David Willcocks

During the Signing of the Register, then shall be sung

Aria
Let the bright Seraphim in burning row,
Their loud uplifted angel-trumpets blow;
Let the Cherubic host, in tuneful choirs,
Touch their immortal harps with golden wires.
Chorus
Let the celestial concerts all unite,
Ever to sound his praise in endless morn of light.

Music George Frideric Handel from 'Samson'

After the Signing of the Register a Fanfare shall be sounded and there shall be played

Pomp and Circumstance No. 4 in G .... *Edward Elgar*
Crown Imperial .... *William Walton*

The Dean introduced the service and soon the Archbishop of Canterbury, with firm solemnity, took the couple through their vows. The Prince continued to look reassuringly at his bride. She seemed now to be quite nervous, but once or twice smiled back at him. He said 'I will' with some feeling. Lady Diana's 'I will' was high and clear. Throughout their fingers were intertwined.

At the weddings of the Queen, Princess Margaret and Princess Anne, the marriage service in the 1662 Prayer Book had been used and all three had promised 'to obey'. Lady Diana and Prince Charles, for their wedding, had chosen an amalgam of the Church of England Series I marriage service and prayers from the new Alternative Service Book.

As the Prince made his wedding vows, he concentrated with anxious attention on the Archbishop's words, repeating after him: 'I, Charles Philip Arthur George take thee Diana Frances to my wedded wife, to have and to hold from this day forward, for better for worse, for richer for poorer, in sickness and in health, to love and to cherish, till death us do part, according to God's holy law; and thereto I give thee my troth.' Outside, the crowds, listening to loudspeakers, cheered each set of vows, and could be heard within the cathedral.

In speaking her vows, in a clear but nervous monotone, Lady Diana reversed the order of the Prince's first two names. Then as if in sympathy, the Prince omitted a word from his vows and altered another when he placed the wedding ring on the fourth finger of her left hand. 'All thy goods with thee I share,' he said.

The ring, made of 22-carat gold by Collingwood's of Conduit Street in London, Royal Warrant Holders to the Queen, was fashioned from a nugget of gold found more than fifty years before at Clogau St David's mine in North Wales. The nugget had also been used for the wedding rings of the Queen Mother (1923), the Queen (1947), Princess Margaret (1960), and Princess Anne (1973). The little that was left formed the band that Lady Diana now wore.

They knelt; the congregation still stood. The Archbishop offered prayers for the couple's happiness, that they might 'remain in perfect love and peace together' and then, after joining their right hands together, he pronounced them man and wife. From that moment, the Lady Diana Spencer became the Princess of Wales.

It was just after 11.15. The bride and groom seated themselves on stools as Earl Spencer's arm was taken by his son, who then assisted him to his seat beside

The Archbishop of Canterbury, Dr Robert Runcie, in his new cope, takes the couple through their vows. Lady Diana's three former flatmates can be seen in the first row of the congregation to the right of the picture.

Mrs Shand Kydd. His courage and determination would see him through the day. The choirs of St Paul's and Her Majesty's Chapels Royal then sang a new anthem by the Welsh composer, William Mathias. The Lesson that followed, I Corinthians 13, was read by the Speaker of the House of Commons from a lectern at the edge of the choir and near the bride's family.

From here, the Archbishop of Canterbury now addressed the congregation. He began: 'Here is the stuff of which fairy tales are made: the Prince and Princess on their wedding day. But fairy tales usually end at this point . . . This is not the christian view. Our faith sees the wedding day not as the place of arrival, but the place where the adventure really begins.' He continued: 'Those who are married live happily ever after the wedding day if they persevere in the real adventure which is the royal task of creating each other and creating a more loving world . . . All of us are given the power to make the future more in God's image and to be kings and queens of love. This is our prayer for Charles and Diana. May the burdens we lay on them be matched by the love with which we support them in the years to come.'

Another anthem, 'I was glad' was sung by the choirs as the Prince and Princess of Wales moved up the choir to the high altar. They and the congregation knelt for prayers and for the responses. Brief prayers were then spoken before the altar by Lord Coggan, a former Archbishop of Canterbury, by Cardinal Hume, by the Moderator of the Church of Scotland and by the Rev. Harry Williams, formerly Dean of Prince Charles's college in Cambridge. The latter referred to the bride, for the first time, as 'Diana, Princess of Wales'.

The service drew to its conclusion. The stately hymn, 'I vow to thee, my country', chosen by the bride, preceded the final blessing by the Archbishop, the sung 'Amen', and the National Anthem which was given a superb new setting by Sir David Willcocks.

It was now time for the signing of the register. Dr Runcie led the bride and groom through the sanctuary gates into the south aisle; Lady Sarah Armstrong-Jones still attended the Princess. Thither the Dean and Chapter of St Paul's also conducted the Queen, her husband, her mother, daughter and her other two sons. They were followed by Earl Spencer, Mrs Shand Kydd and Lady Fermoy. While the register was being signed, an aria and a chorus from Handel's oratorio, 'Samson' were sung by the New Zealand soprano, Miss Kiri Te Kanawa, and the Bach Choir.

The Royal Family and the bride's family returned to their seats via the south aisle. Then a triumphant fanfare, played by the State Trumpeters far up in the Whispering Gallery, hailed the return of the bride and the groom to the choir, she with her veil now raised. Happily smiling and talking to each other, they advanced to the dais. Just before they reached it, the full orchestra, conducted by Sir Colin Davis, began playing the resplendent music of Elgar's 'Pomp and Circumstance March' No. 4 in G. On the dais the Prince and Princess of Wales turned towards the Queen: the Prince inclined his head and the Princess made a low curtsy. Turning, she smiled at her mother, and the couple, facing the congregation for the first time, walked hand on hand through the colourful assembly, the bride looking very young and vulnerable. They were followed by the attendants and in due course by the Royal Family, Earl Spencer walking with the Queen – a democratic innovation – and Mrs Shand Kydd with the Duke of Edinburgh. 'I want everyone to come out having had a marvellous, musical and emotional experience', the Prince had said beforehand. And so it was.

Opposite: The Prince and Princess of Wales at the high altar of St Paul's Cathedral when prayers were said by representatives of four different churches.

Right: The Prince of Wales bows while the Princess curtsies to the Queen at the start of their procession down the aisle after their marriage service.

A tumultuous reception greeted the couple as they emerged from the West Door of St Paul's at 12.10. A peal of twelve bells rang out in the northwest tower above them, answered by the sonorous clang of the 17-ton bell, Great Paul, in the southwest tower and by other carillons from church bells in the City. The joyous cheering of the crowds was sustained, and would stay with the couple as they drove in the 1902 State Postillion Landau back to Buckingham Palace, with a golden horseshoe, a gift from the Royal Mews, reposing on the seat before them, and two detectives disguised as footmen behind them. The attendants, with Prince Edward, followed in Queen Alexandra's State Coach and the Glass Coach. Then came the Queen's Carriage Procession.

By 12.40, both processions had entered the inner quadrangle of the Palace, where the warm applause and cheers of the Household staff welcomed them

Opposite: The Prince and Princess of Wales walk down the nave of St Paul's followed by the bridesmaids and pages.

Right: The procession out of St Paul's Cathedral of the Queen with Earl Spencer, followed by the Duke of Edinburgh and the Hon. Mrs Shand Kydd, the Lord Chamberlain to the Queen Mother, and Queen Elizabeth the Queen Mother.

Below: Prince Charles and his bride emerging from St Paul's Cathedral after their marriage service. They are followed by the bridesmaids and pages.

Opposite: The Royal Couple face the world as the Prince and Princess of Wales.

Right: The bridesmaids in taffeta dresses leaving St Paul's Cathedral followed by the two pages in Naval Cadet uniforms, and the supporters – Prince Edward followed by Prince Andrew.

Below left: The Queen with members of the Royal Family and the bride's family at the top of the steps of St Paul's Cathedral after the wedding of Prince Charles and Lady Diana.

Below right: The Prince and Princess of Wales begin their journey from St Paul's to Buckingham Palace along the route lined with crowds of people.

home. The guests attending the wedding breakfast entered the Palace through a side entrance, for The Mall was a tide of humanity being eased forward in waves by lines of police. The bridal party now assembled in the Centre Room on the first floor, before the great glass doors onto the balcony were opened by footmen in response to the singing and chanting of the hundreds of thousands below: 'We want Charlie!' 'We want Di!' And then, when at 1.10 the couple appeared, a new heart-felt anthem arose

Above: Prince Charles kisses his bride on the balcony of Buckingham Palace.

Left: The Royal Family, bridesmaids and pages also appeared with the Prince and Princess on the balcony before the wedding breakfast.

from the crowd – 'You'll never walk alone.' It was as though England had won the Ashes and the World Cup on the same day.

There were four balcony appearances by the royal pair, the attendants, and their families. The masses of people below, who somehow managed not to trample the wide beds of red geraniums, sang 'Rule Britannia' and called for the Queen and the Queen Mother. On the last appearance, encouraged by Prince Andrew, Prince Charles gave his beautiful bride a kiss.

At 1.22, the balcony appearances came to an end, and the couple retired below to receive their guests. But to the delighted surprise of the crowds, they returned to the balcony exactly an hour later, this time with just the Duke of Edinburgh and the Queen.

The wedding breakfast, held in the Ball Supper Room, was attended by 118 of the closest friends and relatives of the Prince and Princess. They sat down at twelve round tables for a three-course luncheon, prepared by the Palace kitchens. There was brill coated in lobster sauce, *suprême de volaille Princesse de Galles*, and strawberries and cream; and three fine

It was too difficult for the police who lined the route not to share the enthusiasm of the crowds.

The hexagonal wedding cake was five feet high and weighed 225 pounds. It was made by the Royal Navy's Cookery School, HMS 'Pembroke', at Chatham.

wines were served. The five-tiered, hexagonal wedding cake had pride of place. It was cut by Prince Charles, using his ceremonial sword. His brothers jointly proposed a toast and the Prince replied.

At 4.20 p.m., the Prince and his bride, showered by rose petals and confetti, left the inner quadrangle of the Palace in an open landau, festooned at the rear with bunches of blue and silver balloons and bearing a large placard on which was scrawled in red 'Just Married'. The couple looked contented and relaxed, and seemed to wonder at the continued affectionate cheering of the crowds lining the route to Waterloo Station.

They were driven right into the station and alongside Platform 12, where a special three-carriage train awaited them, its engine, 73142, was called *Broadlands*. They said goodbye to Lord Maclean who had organized all the wedding ceremonies – the Princess rewarded him with a kiss. Then the couple entered the third carriage. At 4.40, ten minutes late, the train set off on the eighty-mile journey to Romsey in Hampshire.

There, soon after 6.00 p.m. they arrived, and with the minimum of ceremony at the Prince's request, and no red carpet, they were driven through the flag-waving crowds packing the sunny streets. Less than a mile further on they passed through the gates of Broadlands, the family home of the Mountbattens. The eighteenth-century mansion had been closed to the public since 27 July and temporarily vacated by its present owners, Lord and Lady Romsey. Princess Elizabeth and Lieutenant Philip Mountbatten had spent the first week of *their* honeymoon at Broadlands in November 1947, occupying the Portico and Green Rooms which overlook the River Test. For the next three nights, secluded in the 6,000-acre estate, the Queen's eldest son and his young wife would at last have the chance to rest, to adjust themselves to their novel marital state.

Opposite: The bride and groom pose alone at Buckingham Palace after their wedding ceremony.

Overleaf: The Prince and Princess of Wales posing with their families for an official photograph at Buckingham Palace.
Back row (left to right): Captain Mark Phillips, Prince Andrew, Viscount Linley, The Duke of Edinburgh, Prince Edward, the bride and groom, Ruth, Lady Fermoy (bride's grandmother), Lady Jane Fellowes (bride's sister), Viscount Althorp (bride's brother) and Mr Robert Fellowes.
Middle row (left to right): Princess Anne, Princess Margaret, The Queen Mother, The Queen, India Hicks, Lady Sarah Armstrong-Jones (both bridesmaids), Mrs Frances Shand Kydd (bride's mother), Earl Spencer, Lady Sarah McCorquodale (bride's sister) and Mr Neil McCorquodale.
Front row (left to right): Bride's attendants – Edward van Cutsem, Clementine Hambro, Catherine Cameron, Sarah Jane Gaselee and Lord Nicholas Windsor.

On the afternoon of Saturday, 1 August, the Prince and Princess of Wales flew in an Andover of the Queen's Flight, piloted by the Prince, from Eastleigh Airport, Southampton, to Gibraltar, where they joined the Royal Yacht, *Britannia*, and her crew of twenty-two officers and 254 other ranks. The next part of their honeymoon would be spent cruising in the Mediterranean. At the conclusion of the voyage, which would include a visit to Malta, they would fly back to Britain and join the rest of the Royal Family at Balmoral.

In the two months after the wedding, the Prince and his Princess would be able, for the first time, to enjoy each other's company to the full, to get to know each other with the minimum of distractions and duties of social and official engagements. They would need that time to build the sure and lasting foundations of the loving friendship between them that must endure for the rest of their lives.

'A lot of people have a false idea about love,' the Prince once said. 'I think it's more than just a romantic idea of falling madly in love with someone and having a love affair for the rest of your life. It's much more than that – it's a very strong friendship... shared interests and ideas in common, plus a great deal of affection . . . Essentially you must be good friends; and love, I'm sure will grow out of that friendship... I hope I will be as lucky as my parents... To me, marriage, which may be for fifty years, seems to be one of the biggest and most responsible steps to be taken in one's life . . . And marriage isn't only for the two people who form the marriage – it's also for the children.'

Those children may well one day make history in the Royal Family. For among the close relations of the Princess of Wales' family there have been no less than four sets of twins, two pairs of which were identical. Is it possible that the next heir to the throne might be one of such a pair?

The Prince and Princess of Wales crossing Westminster Bridge on the way to Waterloo Station at the start of their honeymoon. The bride wore a coral pink dress of silk tussore and a tricorn hat with pink ostrich feathers.

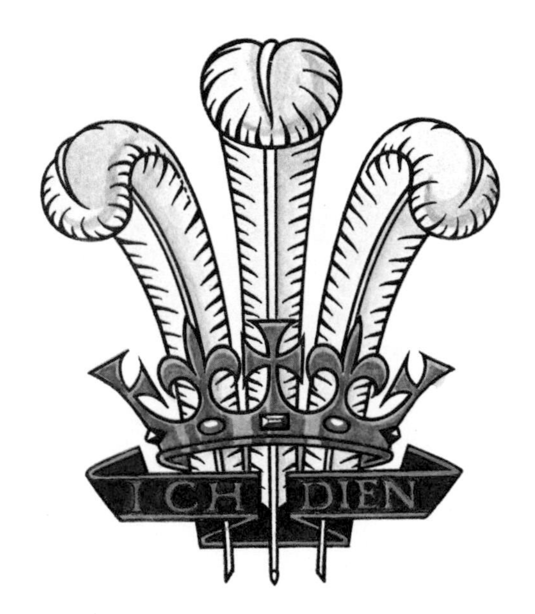
ICH DIEN